THE Last Petal FALLING
A Memoir

Lori Arnold McFarlane

2015

Trade Paperback Edition
Copyright © 2015 by Lori Arnold McFarlane
All rights reserved.

This book or any portion thereof may not be reproduced or used in any manner whatsoever without the express written permission of the publisher except for the use of brief quotations in a book review. Published in the United States by Lori Arnold McFarlane.

ISBN-13: 978-1511899000

Unless otherwise noted, Scripture quotations are taken from the Holy Bible, New International Version®, NIV®. Copyright © 1973, 1978, 1984, 2011 by Biblica, Inc.™ Used by permission of Zondervan. All rights reserved worldwide. www.zondervan.com The "NIV" and "New International Version" are trademarks registered in the United States Patent and Trademark Office by Biblica, Inc.™

Scripture quotations marked (KJV) are taken from the King James Version. *The Holy Bible, King James Version.* Cambridge Edition: 1769; *King James Bible Online,* 2015. http://www.kingjamesbibleonline.org/.

All quoted Scripture verified for accuracy at: "BibleGateway.com: A Searchable Online Bible in over 100 ..." Web. 27 Apr. 2015. <https://www.biblegateway.com/>.

Lyrics gratefully reprinted with permission:
Quiet Company. *We Are All Where We Belong.* Quiet Company, 2012. MP3.

Other publications referred to in this book:
Harris, Joshua. *I Kissed Dating Goodbye.* Sisters, Or.: Multnomah, 1997. Print.
Endo, Shusaku. *Silence.* New York: Taplinger Pub., 1979. Print.
Burnett, John. "For An Ex-Christian Rocker, Faith Lost Is A Following Gained." *NPR.* NPR, 5 Dec. 2013. Web. 6 Dec. 2013. <http://www.npr.org/2013/12/05/247338182/for-an-ex-christian-rocker-faith-lost-is-a-following-gained>.

First Edition
Cover Design by Lori Arnold McFarlane

Some names and identifying details have been changed to respect and protect the privacy of individuals.

To Fi, Lolly, and Jaguar
And of course Scott

> "We search through the shadows of our souls
> to try and tame the demons we control,
> and searching for a god we'll never know."
>
> -Quiet Company, "Never Tell Me the Odds"
> *We Are All Where We Belong*

Part 1
Before

Chapter 1
Elementary Evangelist

In Memory of Corduroy
The grave clouds are the gray corduroy skirt
I wore every Tuesday, Chapel Day,
when I was ten.
Chapel with its dim lights and songs and prayers
shadowed my friendlessness like a friend.
I fit in with Mary and Jesus
who also wore homemade dresses
and messy hair.
The stained glass masked my stained
corduroy skirt, and praising the Lord
lifted my eyes over the pulpit
across the altar into the baptismal.

MANY PEOPLE SAY "I'VE BEEN a Christian all my life." What that exactly means, however, is different for everyone. Does it mean I've gone to church since I was a child? Been raised in the South where everyone is a so-called Christian? Or does it mean I've been a conscious believer for as long as I can remember?

I can't remember a time when I didn't believe in Jesus as my Savior. I "asked Jesus into my heart" and was baptized when I was ten. I "rededicated my life" when I was eighteen. Through a life less than perfect I tripped and stumbled towards the God I had always known, always trusted, always loved.

Even from a very young age, I was very religious. I felt led to witness whenever an opportunity came up; in fact, I used to *make* the opportunity come up with a special formula. In elementary school, when I made a friend at the swimming pool or in the park, I attempted to lead our conversation (and possibly my unsaved new friend) to the Lord by asking a pre-planned series of three specific questions: *What school do you go to? Is that a Christian school? Are you a Christian?* If the final answer was no, I then attempted to tell them how they could become one.

On one very memorable occasion, my friends and I met a strange boy in their neighborhood causing a little mischief by trying to pull what looked like a pipe out of the ground. I used my formula on him and discovered he was not a Christian. Feeling heavily that it was our duty to bring him to Christ, my friends and I went home to prepare a missionary parade. We pulled out the construction paper, markers, scissors, and Elmer's glue to design banners and flags to wave, as well as picture booklets with pull-out flaps which told the stories of the Bible. Our outreach materials weren't about Jesus and his death and resurrection - you know, *the Gospel* - but rather Jonah And The Whale, Noah's Ark, David and Goliath, and Joshua And The Battle of Jericho. I guess we felt these stories were as pertinent as any for one's salvation. The whole Bible is God's true word and therefore necessary for life everlasting, right?

We then gathered our materials and marched up and down the street, singing *Jesus Loves Me* and *Jesus Loves the Little Children,* in hopes of rousing the boy's attention and interest. Sadly, he was already long gone by the time the glue had dried on our artwork.

I was a little over-zealous for a second-grader, I suppose. And I was certainly a goody two-shoes.

I had been in church my whole life and in Christian schools since kindergarten. I believed in Jesus with my whole heart and tried my best to do right. Aside from talking too much, I never got in trouble (at school anyway– at home, my mother probably remembers me as quite a bit less well-behaved.) When the other kids broke the rules, I was the not-so-silent conscientious objector. At one particular slumber party when I was twelve, I voiced my disapproval of my friends' choice of VHS rental and stoically sat by myself for an hour and a half in the bedroom while the rest of the girls watched the forbidden PG-13 rated movie in the living room. Sure my mom may never have found out, but God would know. I wasn't allowed to watch certain cartoons either, so I always requested *Ghostbusters* and *Smurfs* be turned off while visiting friends' homes. I was annoyingly obedient in those types of situations. This did not win me a very rewarding reputation.

At school, I was in the out-crowd. The other outcasts were nice to me and happily sat with me at lunch and invited me to sleep overs, but I wanted to be loved by everyone. I wanted to be popular. I tried my hardest fit in. At school – and church – I carefully studied how others acted and reacted in every circumstance so I could be like them. I paid close attention to what jokes made the class laugh and which ones fell flat. I analyzed what made the jokes funny, completely missing the point that delivery, and more importantly, *deliverer*, were the main ingredients for classroom laughter. I watched how they teased each other, and how that was different from the way they made fun of others.

I scrutinized the way they looked at me during recess or group activities to discern what they really thought of me. I tried so hard to be like them. Every year at the end of the school term at our little private school, we had an awards ceremony. Along with academic and athletic awards, the school awarded one student in every class the "Best Christian Conduct" award. Each student voted for the kid in his or her class who most deserved the title, making it more of a popularity contest than it should've been. I wanted that title and that little gold and marble plaque more than anything. In fifth grade, I practically campaigned for it. Fifth grade was the year I had my first and only elementary school boyfriend, Zeke. He was in the popular, bad-boy group, but he was also a little odd, like me. I told him how desperately I wanted that award. He then told all his friends to vote for me for that year, and for the first time, and last, I got it. My Best Christian Conduct plaque sat on my bookshelf for the rest of my school days as one of my most prized trophies.

I thought endlessly about God and heaven and salvation. I asked Jesus into my heart on several occasions, never really sure if the last time had been genuine enough. I knew that I was a sinner and could never be good enough to get to heaven without accepting Jesus' death on the cross. I also knew it was my job as a Christian to warn others of the consequences. I brought a little boy in my first grade class to tears when I lead the crusade of six year old interventionists to surround him and inform him that he was *not* perfect like his mother kept telling him he was but was a sinner who needed Jesus!

Among the many times I asked Jesus in to my heart, the one that I would consider the "real" one for many years to come was when I was ten. I was lying in my bed late one summer night listening to the Christian singer Carmen on my cassette player. His words moved me, and I knew then and there that I needed Jesus to wash me of my sins. I laid down on the floor at the threshold of my bedroom door, body prone on the carpet with just my face lying on the cold green hallway linoleum, and I asked Jesus into my heart. I felt different after that, and believed for years (until I went to college) that *that* was the moment I was saved.

I wanted to be baptized next. Our church pastor met with me to discuss my decision to be baptized to make sure I knew what I was doing. Even as a ten year old, I was extremely excited about having a theological discussion with a real actual pastor. I was ready to discuss what baptism meant, talk about the Bible, ask and answer questions… and I was heavily disappointed when all he did was ask me if I believed in Jesus and had asked him into my heart. I didn't even get to tell him the story of how I was saved. The meeting was over almost as quickly as it began, and I was baptized in front of the church two weeks later. I never even got to ask my questions about how I could be sure I wouldn't lose my salvation if I sinned (which I knew I still did) and how I could always know that I was definitely going to heaven.

For even at that age, I was interested in theology and though I never admitted it to anyone, I was perplexed by several subjects, the most perplexing being how we knew we could not lose our salvation. My church taught that we could not, and I remember my dad assuring me of it, but I did not know *for sure* how it could be so sure. I wondered if I could ever sin so badly that my salvation would be taken away from me. What if I did something bad and got killed in a car wreck before I had time to repent? I used to have conversations about this with my cousin Nate, who told me he would often lie in bed at night listening for the trumpet blast signifying the Second Coming. He told me he asked Jesus into his heart every night before he went to bed just to make sure. I knew this wasn't right (my dad had told me it wasn't), but a part of me worried too. Hell was too dangerous to mess around with and heaven too good to miss…

Heaven also perplexed me. It really was too good. When I imagined it, and imagined myself surrounded by all white and light, doing nothing but singing "*Glory, glory, glory, hallelujah*" to Jesus for ever and ever and ever, I was burdened by a sense of absolute total boredom. It seemed like a really, extremely long time to be doing the same thing over and over. It gave me the same feeling in my stomach as lying on my back on the grass in my front yard and staring up into the endless blue sky – a feeling like I was falling and would never stop falling, a sense of dread in my core.

Any time this feeling hit me, I immediately asked God to forgive me for having such awful thoughts. The fact that I felt that way must be a reflection of my sinfulness. *Of course praising God for eternity is going to be great!* I tried to convince myself.

Also perplexing to me was the Rapture. Like probably all evangelical kids, I experienced numerous times the cold-sweat moments of "*Did the Rapture just come and I got left behind?!*" If I came home to a silent, empty house, having expected my parents to be there, I immediately assumed, with heat radiating under my arms, that they'd been raptured and I hadn't. If I couldn't get my mom or dad to answer their work phones or my grandparents next door to answer their home phone, and then in a panic, any of my friends to answer *their* phones, I came unglued, thinking for sure I'd been left behind. I never knew how I could know for sure I was definitely saved. It all seemed too risky, too much riding on that one detail that I felt I had so little control over. I was sure I had Jesus in my heart, and knew I meant it and believed it, but was it really enough? Did I *really* love God enough, or was I just fooling myself?

I had really looked forward to talking to that real life actual pastor.

Chapter 2
The Summer of Flies

THE SUMMER BEFORE SEVENTH GRADE my family moved to a new town, and I started public school. It was a culture-shock, going from a small Christian private elementary school to a large public junior high. I thought the "bad" kids in my old school had been rebellious, but my new peers were downright *sinful*. Unlike my "bad" Christian classmates, these new schoolmates smoked, swore, and didn't go to church. They wore ripped up, tatty clothes and oversized black skull T-shirts instead of expensive boutique clothes like the rich private school kids. The popular girls were all volleyball players and cheerleaders. I didn't know how to assimilate this new culture into the system I'd so painstakingly studied. I didn't know where I belonged in this new social hierarchy. Rich, preppy kids were still popular, but "stoners and thugs" were just as intimidating.

To my incredible luck, I discovered on my first morning that my locker was right next to Leah's, my old best friend from kindergarten. We were both new to the school and relieved to find each other. From the start, I had a partner with whom I would brave the unkind jungle that is public junior high.

I made another new friend on the first day in my English class. Her name was Heather. I introduced Heather and Leah, and we became the Three Musketeers. Leah was a Christian like me, but Heather wasn't. Heather's home life was vastly different from ours – divorced parents, mother living with a boyfriend, both smokers, but I soon learned to accept all that. Young people are highly adaptable.

Seventh grade was a new world for all of us. While I still clung to my good Christian values and reverently attended church every Sunday, my friends were discovering the excitement of little rebellious acts like smoking cigarettes. They found solidarity in the stoner crowd, and by extension, that's where I ended up too. Huddled after lunch outside in the smoking circles, I always passed the cigarette. I ate lunch with the stoners and pretended to be one of them, but I knew once again I just didn't fit in.

A few years previously, a teenaged girl that I admired from church gave a presentation on a mission trip she had been on with Teen Missions International (TMI). It looked amazing, going to far away exotic countries without my parents to do missionary work for an entire summer. The summer after sixth grade I went on a Pre-teen trip to Venezuela, and that following summer I signed up for an eight-week Teen summer mission trip to Pakistan. It sounds ludicrous now to take a team of thirty-two teenagers, ranging from ages thirteen to twenty-one, to Pakistan, and it wasn't much less radical in 1995. People thought my parents were crazy, but my parents trusted the organization and believed in its cause. I chose a team that would run a two-week TMI style "Boot Camp" training course with local Pakistani Christian teens in the then still developing town of Gujranwala (now one of the largest, most prosperous industrial cities in the country) and afterwards build a car garage for a local Christian mechanic in Jhelum. People could not come into the country as Christian missionaries but were permitted as tourists who might volunteer their time helping Christians already living there. We weren't allowed to do any proselytizing but could encourage those Christians already struggling as the religious minority in a Muslim nation.

So at the end of my seventh grade school year, I packed my TMI-issued duffel bag with my TMI-supplied list of necessities – work gloves, bug spray, laundry detergent, a brand new green leather Bible with my name embossed in gold, a little bottle of malaria pills - and I caught the cross-country TMI bus to Florida at the Memphis pick-up. Boot Camp is the first leg of a TMI summer mission. For the first two weeks, we slept in tents on a rainy, mosquito-infested island just off the coast of Cocoa Beach. We woke up every morning at 5:30, had breakfast, and then before settling down for daily private devotions, ran a high intensity Obstacle Course (OC) which included feats like rope swinging over a muddy "Slough of Despond" water pit, climbing the twenty-five foot high cargo net "Jacob's Ladder", and scaling a twelve foot wall with only hands and feet and the assistance of other teammates. The OC's purpose was to prepare us physically and mentally for the difficult challenges ahead on all our various mission fields, whether it be evangelizing while backpacking Mt Kilimanjaro, volunteering in an AIDS orphanage in Africa, building a hospital in Papua New Guinea, or in our case, constructing a large concrete work shed in Pakistan. We took classes in bricklaying, concrete mixing, steel-tying, and witnessing. Boot Camp was miserable but what the leaders called "character building". The rules are tremendously rigid, and every slight misstep – a whisper while lining up, tardiness, a messy tent, a dress code error – warranted the affectionately labeled punishment "Special Blessing" (SB), or in other words, physical labor during our free time. (Because discipline, they said, is a blessing!) One would think we should all hate Boot Camp, but most of us loved it... or so we said when we all arrived back home at the end of the summer and were feeling nostalgic. It was fun, in its own sadistic way. Following our two weeks of training, all the different teams boarded planes for their various international destinations, duffel bags full of our meager personal belongings, enough food to last us all summer, and all of our own work tools.

I was the youngest person on the Pakistan team, one of only two thirteen year olds. I was extremely immature compared to the eighteen, nineteen and twenty year olds. I didn't like washing my own clothes in a bucket. I wore the same dirty socks for days and days without a mother to do my laundry for me. I still had that weird sense of humor but now also a "bad girl" persona that I thought made me kind of cool. I said a few swear words. I was utterly boy-crazy. I was irresponsible and moody. I was, actually, a typical thirteen year old.

Boot Camp had prepared us for many of the Pakistani idiosyncrasies we would encounter. We girls were taught not to look men or boys in the eyes, we kept our hair covered in long scarves and wore *shalwar kameez*, the long sleeved, full-length tunics over loose trousers worn by Pakistanis, to avoid offending anyone with our Western immodesty. We had learned how to perform daily work tasks, and we took turns doing Kitchen Patrol (KP) preparing the days' meals. It was monsoon season, so we had the relief of escaping our work and the intense heat every afternoon for indoor Bible Study. We took cold showers (a luxury after bathing in a bucket for two weeks at Boot Camp) and boiled water for drinking.

One miserably hot morning, Kara, a fifteen year old, and I were on KP. It was in between breakfast and lunch time, and we were given an hour's free time to write letters home. The girls stayed in an empty two bedroom concrete cube, sleeping in sleeping bags lined up in rows on the floor. Our little dormitory was surrounded on all sides by a ten-foot brick wall and a lockable door, with an enclosed open air atrium between the building and the outer door. Kara and I closed the dormitory door and immediately stripped down to shorts and tank tops in the privacy of our own secluded space to write our letters and cool off from the scorching mid-morning heat.

But we had forgotten to lock the outer gate.

We were both engrossed in our letter writing when we heard our door open. We looked up, expecting to see a fellow teammate. Instead we were alarmed to see an unfamiliar middle-aged Pakistani man hovering at the door and leering at us American girls exposing so much skin.

In broken English he said, "I have come for a drink of water." I couldn't speak for fright, and Kara barely managed to stutter, "There – there's a – a spigot outside." He advanced towards us. I was cornered, and he put his large, rough hands on my bare white thigh to caress. Silently I cried out to Jesus to help us as Kara crept out the door and coaxed, "Here, uh, sir, I'll give you some water, here, this spigot- out- side." The man turned to gape at her bare freckled shoulders now gleaming in the sunlight.

I darted away from him and joined Kara. He followed us into the outside atrium. Kara boldly stepped outside the walled gate and pointed to the nonexistent "spigot". I stayed in the atrium, reading her mind and ready to act. The man prowled out the gate, his disbelieving eyes still all over Kara's half-naked body. She instantly, stealthily, doubled back, slammed the gate over, and locked it with trembling fingers. With the man safely outside, Kara and I dashed back into the dormitory building and locked that door too. We then fell apart in each other's arms.

The trauma of the experience was overpowering, but even more terrifying was going to be the part where we confessed what happened to our leaders. We had been incautious, and who knows what almost happened to us because of it? After our break was over, and we were safely fully dressed again, we crept out of our compound, still clinging to each other, and speedily made our way back to the kitchen. When we told our head female leader what happened to us, we received no hugs, no pity, just a fresh telling off for our inattention to the rules.

I thanked God profusely that night for protecting us in spite of our irresponsibility.

We had six leaders in charge of us. The two senior leaders, Pam and Sam, rhyming names, were a stuffy English couple who took an immediate disliking to me. I was probably a little difficult to handle. That's not to say I didn't try though. I may have seen myself as a little bad and daring after a year at the stoner table, but in reality, I was still almost perfectly squeaky clean. I was simply a hormonal thirteen year old who didn't like doing my own laundry. At the end of the day, despite my mood swings and sometimes bad attitude, I would never have agreed to do anything immoral or intentionally sinful. I did end up with a sort of boyfriend on the team, which is a major TMI rulebreaker. Still, even though we gave each other little notes declaring affection for each other in innocently spiritual terms (*I pray for you daily*, or *In Christ's love, I-sign-my-name*), and even though we sat together at lot on buses and at meal times, we never held hands or kissed or did any of the actual boyfriend/girlfriend stuff. We got split up repeatedly. For days at a time we were forbidden to speak to each other. The older girls on the team, particularly Jan, took me under their wing and were wonderful to me, and tried to help me understand why this rule existed. I tried not to "pair off", but I couldn't help it. I was friends with nearly everyone on the team, but any conversation lasting longer than a few minutes with Tim was picked on by my leaders, and we'd be separated again. I also got in trouble repeatedly for "pairing off" with the only other thirteen year old on the team, Laura. She and I were instant best friends, but even best friends were prohibited. I spent a lot of time separated from the two people I cared most about.

I wasn't trying to break the rules. I never tried to break the rules - not until one weekend when our team took a special break and visited the tourist city of Murree on the southern slopes of the Western Himalayans. Only three of the assistant leaders, Janine, Dave, and Bret, accompanied us there. (Michael, our sixth leader, was hardly ever in sight. I barely remember him.) TMI has a lot of strict rules about how team members behave and look not only at Boot Camp, but out on the field. We had to wear eight-inch tall army boots at all times (hence "Boot" Camp), making us stick out like crazy American thumbs everywhere we went. Besides the no-pairing-off rule, there were others like no secular music, no discussing theology, no piercings (other than one set of earrings on ladies), no sleeveless tops or skirts that showed the knee – not exactly a problem for *our* well-covered team, of course. Yet, while we were in Murree, the rules all seemed to relax a little, with our stuffy English leaders out of the picture. We stayed in a Western Christian boarding school for missionary children, and spent the evenings in the common room listening to Snoop Doggy Dogg, Nirvana, and Beck. We hung out in bedrooms of the opposite sex playing cards (two more rules broken). Everyone was involved; I recall no one abstaining from the harmless debauchery.

One afternoon, in my dorm room with Laura, Tim, and another guy Trevor, someone suggested we play strip poker. It was silly. We removed socks and boots and hair bows, and that was it. Not so much as a hairless boy's chest was revealed; I was far too prude to go any further. After our silly game ended, I headed back to the common room for some more forbidden secular music and dancing (so many broken rules) with other members of the team.

We returned to Jhelum and our project. Our project was to build a car garage for a local mechanic. We mixed and poured concrete, we dug holes, and we broke bricks with hammers. We wore hard hats and boots and *shalwar kameez*. We drank water by the canteenful and sweated and suffered heat rash. Building this car shed for our mechanic missionary was hard labor, but we loved it. We had fun testing the limits of our youthful bodies. We fought over who got to turn the enormous cement mixer. We laughed and chased each other and sang praise songs while we worked. We had a higher mission; we were working for the glory of God.

During the afternoon monsoons, we stayed indoors for Bible Study and laundry and shower time. In the breezy mornings, before the sun blazed too hot, we had our devos.

Daily private devotions, "devos", were an integral part of the Teen Missions experience. Every morning, before breakfast, we broke up for devos. For thirty minutes, we sat alone, in any inspirational and comfortable place we could find for silent reflection, prayer, and Scripture reading. I loved devos. I felt they brought me closer to the Lord... except for when they put me to sleep. I found it so hard to stay awake so early in the morning, silently reading the Bible and praying in my head on an empty stomach. I often found it hard to know what to read or pray about. Many times I asked for forgiveness for falling asleep, or for wanting to fall asleep. I found if I moved very far away from the rest of the crowd, I could whisper my prayers, and that kept me awake. I was distracted by all the flies. If you sit still for any length of time in Pakistan, you will be quite literally covered in resting flies. I got used to it, but when they covered my Bible, it was hard to read for all the swatting. I was also terrified to put my Bible down. I'd been chastised by a Pakistani pastor for doing devos with my Bible on the floor, a highly disrespectful way to treat God's Word in their culture. I couldn't show the bottoms of my feet either – another cultural taboo – so finding a place to sit on the ground, with my Bible elevated, the soles of my boots facing down, and my *shalwar kameez* discreet, I was never very comfortable. It was still remarkably conducive to sleep though.

When I wasn't nodding off, however, I was growing closer to Jesus. I was taking in his words – the Gospels were my favorite – and I was maturing in a slow, honest way. Things that challenged me I really took to heart. I was a child, but when Jesus said hating your brother was as bad as murder, I repented of my hateful feelings towards others.

One particular morning, during devos, I had a wonderful experience. I was praying for God's power, when the sun broke through the clouds and a ray of sunshine poured directly onto me. In my mind's eye, I remember a sunray like a yellow painting, coming from a holy cloud, warming my body and my spirit. I basked in the Holy Spirit's smile, as the cool of the morning burnt off me in tender spiritual warmth. After devos was over, I was eager to share my heavenly experience with the rest of the team. The older girls were thrilled for me. I told my leaders. The younger adults smiled, the careless British ones blew me off.

I don't know how long after that experience the next thing happened. Laura, Tim, Trevor, and I were called up to speak privately with the leaders.

Stuffy Pam asked directly, "Lori. Did you break any rules while you were in Murree?" Baffled as to why I was the only one being called out about this, I stumbled over my answer as the other three looked off into the fly ridden sky.

"Um, yes, ma'am. I, well we, I mean we listened to secular music. We played cards… and we danced." I was blushing horribly with guilt and the embarrassment of being so unfairly singled out.

"Anything else?"

I thought hard. Shamefaced, I added, "Guys were in girls' rooms."

"And?"

I was baffled now. I couldn't remember anything else we'd done. I looked to my friends for help, but all eyes were still wandering.

Sam helped me out. "We have been made aware you were also involved in playing strip poker." Petrified, and afraid I'd looked like I had been lying by omission, I tried to explain.

"We, well, I mean, yes, I guess we did sort of play strip poker, but I mean, we didn't take anything off! I mean, I'm so sorry, I just forgot about that, because we didn't do anything..." No one was giving me any help as Sam and Pam glared down at me.

I was then informed that if we weren't so close to the end of our trip, I and my partners in sin would have been sent home early. My stomach dropped. I burst into tears. *How could I have been so stupid! Of course strip poker is strip poker, even if nothing came off!* I burned with shame.

After the others confirmed my story, they were dismissed. I was held back. Pam watched me coldly as she said in her thick English accent, "I'm sorry, Lori, but I really just don't think you are a Christian."

I turned to leave. My boots dragged through the dirt, too heavy to lift, as I trudged back to my dorm for laundry and shower time. Tears dripped down my tanned face. I was in a fog of misery and injustice. *How dare she tell me I'm not a Christian! All because I did stuff everyone else did too! All because I played a stupid game where I didn't even do anything wrong!* But worse than the mortification and resentment I felt for that mean, terrible woman was the fear that she was right.

What if I'm not a Christian?

But that sun! That light! It had to mean something, right? Or did it? Maybe I was just fooling myself. Back in the dorms, I was comforted by the other girls. I told them what Pam had said to me. Jan, the oldest girl on our team, looked me directly in the eyes and told me to ignore what she had said to me, that she had no right. I hugged her tightly for her kindness, but the damage was already done in my vulnerable young heart.

How could I ever know if I was truly saved?

They forced us to call our parents and tell them what happened. I cried the entire time, so remorseful, so embarrassed, so scared of their reaction. I couldn't even defend myself with an explanation of how innocent it had seemed at the time, because the leaders were standing over me, listening to every word to make sure I didn't tell any lies. My parents reacted with surprise and disappointment, but with a lot more grace than I expected. It wasn't until afterwards that I learned the whole, miserable story, compounding my humiliation all the more. As it turned out, after our little game of stripless poker in my dorm room, the same group got back together later that evening with Tiffany taking my place. In a dark closet, the four played real strip poker and got half-naked together. The rumor had gotten out somehow, and I was placed at the scene of the crime instead of Tiff. How? Because one of our leaders, Bret, had passed by my dorm room that afternoon and peeked in. He saw us playing cards, waved to us, and shrugged it off, untroubled by our double rule breaking. Yet when the rumor of the four kids playing strip poker broke out, Bret remembered what he'd seen in my room. Remembering we were barefoot, he named us the four offenders.

Hence the reason my friends refused to speak up. Not wanting to incriminate Tiffany too, no one admitted there were two games going on, and I was innocent of the indecorous one. I was infuriated by the betrayal, both of concealing my innocence and of Tim seeing two other girls in their bras. Tiff was never punished, but the incident was recorded on my permanent TMI record. (There really is a permanent TMI record.)

I left Pakistan that summer with the disgrace and shame of a depraved thirteen year old non-Christian heathen who never liked to wash her socks. I left with the yoke of uncertainty for where I would be spending the afterlife – in heaven or in hell.

Chapter 3
The Karen Carpenter Year

I DISEMBARKED THE INTERNATIONAL FLIGHT and joyfully greeted my smiling parents. These were the days when non-travelers could come as far as the gate to see you off or welcome you home. I hugged my mom and dad happily, never realizing until then how much I'd missed them. My mom commented on how thin I'd become. Living on rice, naan, and chicken-or-beef for an entire summer, combined with daily physical labor, took about fifteen pounds off my already slim frame.

Oh the pleasure of air conditioning! Soft sheets, my own clean bed! Fresh machine laundered clothes! My shoes! A hot shower! These were the luxuries we voluntarily forewent for eight weeks, and never had I truly appreciated them until now. I would never take fluffy Tide-white socks for granted again! How they cushioned my blistered and calloused feet. I saw Leah the next day and rattled endlessly on about all the wonders I'd seen, all the things we'd done, and how amazing air-conditioning felt. School was already about to start again, and we were excited about ruling junior high as the supreme eighth graders.

I went back to school in a new plaid skirt, white button up shirt, and V-neck sweater vest with knee socks and Mary Janes – the height of early '90s Alicia Silverstone fashion. I wore my new David's star necklace I'd gotten in Israel where we spend our final week "debriefing".

One of our punishments for our sinful little card game was being grounded from sight-seeing at Debrief. Debrief is the last week of a TMI mission trip, where the team travels to a separate destination from where they'd been stationed all summer for lessons on re-entering the normal world, how to share our religious experiences and our faith, and for sight-seeing and relaxation after working hard. Sam and Pam (and presumably Michael, the unseen leader) skipped Debrief and flew back to England, leaving all thirty-two of us under the sole care of Bret, Dave, and Janine. With Pakistan stamped in our passports, we were unable to fly into Israel, so we flew to Jordan and bussed across the border. We stayed a day in Amman, and while the rest of the team toured the country's unfathomable sandy sites, we four were stuck in the hotel with Janine and Arabic TV. We were lucky she even let us watch that, as TV is also forbidden on TMI trips, no matter what language it's in.

Once we drove into Israel and reached Jerusalem, the leaders decided to relax our punishment. Perhaps because they too felt banning children from the once-in-a-lifetime opportunity to walk where Jesus walked was too cruel. Or maybe none of them were willing to miss the chance themselves by being stuck in the dormitories baby-sitting us. Either way, we were permitted to see the sights. We played in the sands of the Sea of Galilee. We visited one of the *many* possible tombs where Jesus might have been buried. (If you'd asked me, the one in view of the possible Skull of the Rock would've been my bet.) We visited the Wailing Wall and Dome of the Rock. We walked down the Via Dolorosa, the street down which Jesus carried his cross. (Still feeling tormented over the state of my soul, I berated myself for not tearing up like Jan did as we walked those sacred cobblestones.) We bought souvenirs and toured museums. I bought my little David's star necklace and wore it with Judeo-Christian pride.

On that first day back to school, friends and faculty alike commented on how much weight I'd lost. I loved the attention. I'd never felt fat before, but all these comments, which I took as compliments, delighted me. I'd never even really thought about my weight until then, though now I realized I really was much skinnier.

I liked the perceived approval. Perhaps it was due to being spiritually broken apart at the end of the trip, or from being repeatedly separated from my closest teammates for pairing off for the entire summer, that the attention piqued my hunger for acceptance and validation. I wanted the comments to keep coming, so I made that happen – by ceasing to buy my school lunches. I used the excuse that I'd forgotten my lunch money. If I was a little hungry, I bummed a French fry off of a friend's plate. At home, I'd say I wasn't hungry, or I'd miss family dinner using homework as an excuse, or I'd push my food around my plate, eating the peas or the mashed potato and leaving the rest. With the actual weight never being the key issue, I never knew how many pounds I was losing, only that my clothes were getting roomier and the comments kept coming. The guidance counsellor mentioned one day to me, "You lose much more, and you'll waste away to nothing!" It was great getting attention.

I was still totally uncool and unpopular, though I continued my attempt to fit in. While Heather and Leah still hung out with the stoners, as did I by proxy, I wasn't friends with any of them. They didn't like me, and I didn't really like them. I told myself I didn't care. I had that year moved into the pre-Advanced Placement classes, full of kids who'd been friends with each other since elementary school through Gifted & Talented. I was now in GT too, but they all thought I was weird because I'd been to Pakistan and assumed I was just another stoner like my friends. I made a few in-class friends, mostly seventh graders, whom I waved to in the corridors but rarely spoke to outside of class, much less school.

By now, Heather and Leah had graduated from mere cigarettes to marijuana and were smoking with their friends after school. I sometimes tagged along but always felt uncomfortable. Mini Thins were also making the rounds, little ephedrine energy pills kids sold to each other, taking multiple doses and claiming the effects were just like speed. My summer away had made me even more virtuous than ever, and I knew all of this was very wrong. I clutched my David's star like it was a cross and wished I could pull my friends back from the precipice of mortal danger.

Eighth grade was the year sex entered our lives. Leah was the first to lose her virginity. Heather was eager to dispose of hers next, by whatever means. I had lots of boyfriends but had barely even kissed most of them, never mind considered sleeping with them. It wasn't even a consideration. I was waiting until marriage. One boyfriend, Doug, lived a few miles down the road from me. We rode the same school bus and kissed a couple of times. We broke up over the phone, but I still had some unresolved feelings for him.

Heather, Leah, and I were forever spending the night at each other's houses, even on school nights. One Friday night, Heather slept over. As it grew closer to midnight and my parents had already gone to bed, Heather told me she wanted to lose her virginity. Tonight. Would I call Doug for her and see if he would meet us at the lake? I was embarrassed, and a little jealous, but very much the push-over best friend, I called him and handed the phone to Heather. She asked if he could sneak out and meet us at the lake between our houses. She told him to bring a condom. She hung up and excitedly ran back to my room to get ready. She borrowed a pair of my black panties, because the ones she was wearing weren't cute enough. Then she pushed open my bedroom window, and we crawled out to meet Doug at the lake.

She was giggling the whole way. I tried to be giggly too, but I was hurt. She was going to have sex with my ex-boyfriend, only broken up days ago! And what was I to do? In the dead of night we sneaked down to the fishing lake a little ways from my house, diving into the ditches with every oncoming headlight. We came to the designated meeting area where Doug was already waiting anxiously.

Heather tried to convince me to go skinny dipping with them, but I said no. I sat on a tree stump some distance away, as the two of them dipped into the cold night water together. I turned to face the other way. I was cold and close to crying. I turned back around to see they were oblivious to me, so I got up and walked back home. I crawled back through my cracked window, shut it tight and went to sleep, secretly hoping Heather wouldn't be able to get back in.

A quiet knock on my window woke me. Though I wanted to leave Heather in the cold, I obediently and best-friendedly opened the window for her. She was buzzing with excitement. She wanted to tell me everything. I pretended to listen to her tale, but hidden from her by the darkness I screwed my eyes shut and tried to go back to sleep. I didn't want to hear it. I didn't want to hear any of it. I was furious, but what could I do? We were the Three Musketeers, and you have to be happy for your friends.

Math and American History were the two classes I didn't take in pre-AP. I hated both of them. Heather was in History with me but sat on the other side of the alphabetically seated classroom. We communicated via notes passed to each other through the messengers in the desks between us. History was right before lunch. On the Monday after Heather's adventure at the lake, she passed me a little note. The bell was going to ring in a few minutes. I surreptitiously unfolded the note under my desk.

Me and Leah have decided that since you're still a virgin, you can't hang out with us anymore. Don't sit with us at lunch. – Heather

I stared at the note. I turned to Heather who was falsely paying rapt attention to the teacher pointing her stick at the blackboard and droning on about the Magna Carta. The bell rang. She was the first out of the classroom, while I sat dumbfounded.

Lunch seatings in junior high are critical. If you ever, ever sit alone, it's social suicide. I now had nowhere to go. Since I didn't eat lunch anyway, I ran to the girls' restroom, to cry alone instead.

Amy and Audrey were putting on their thick black eyeliner and heavy red lipstick when I entered. Amy and Audrey were the infamous school sluts. Whether they were actually sexually active or not, that's what we all called them, and that's what everyone knew them for. I'd never spoken to either of them before, but as soon as I shoved open the door sobbing, they both dropped their make-up bags and threw their arms around me in comfort. It took me a few moments to compose myself enough to tell them what had just happened.

"Well, forget about them. You can be our friend." They were both in perfect agreement and completely genuine. Arms over my shoulders, they walked me to the cafeteria where I sat at their friendless table, always the social outcast. At least I wasn't sitting alone.

Amy and Audrey were my new Best-Friends-Forever at school, but we never spent time together outside the school doors. They were essentially two best friends reaching out to a lost soul, and though they included me honestly and lovingly named me their new best friend, we had nothing in common. I loved them though; they kept me safe from rejection and helped me hold my head high when passing Heather or Leah in the halls.

I felt utterly alone. I started writing dark poetry. I daydreamed about suicide but was afraid of going to hell. I took a few Mini Thins to see if they really did anything, but the guilt of "taking drugs" consumed me. I wrote extensively about blood and death and blackness and bleakness, but also about God and grace and hope, just in case my private writings were ever found and the sincerity of my faith questioned. I told myself no one would notice if I were gone, except maybe my parents. I knew they would be pretty sad, and I loved them and didn't want them to be sad, but the darkness in my heart grew ever darker, and death was the only visible avenue out of it. If only hell weren't so close on the other side, I could just take a whole lot of Mini Thins and be done with it. I knew I could never do it, not really, not when I knew my parents loved me, but I wanted to. I was lonely and empty and dark. In health class, somewhere tucked in between abstinence-only sex education and warnings of the addictive qualities of a dangerous drug called marijuana (also known as *weed* or *Mary Jane*), Coach "Bitchford" remarked that all kids our age felt dark and lonely. But my darkness felt heavier and lonelier than theirs, and I wanted to feel a physical pain that could drown out the echoes and screams of my inner chaos.

I wanted to try cutting myself. I didn't know if it was suicide I was after or just pain, but one afternoon, alone in my house, I was ready to try it. I didn't know how to go about it though, for there was no internet then from which to get instructions, and my life experience was too sheltered to follow advice from fellow cutters. I knew I needed a razor. What kind of a razor? I went to my mom and dad's bathroom and found a plastic shaving razor. Was this it? I held it to my wrist. I didn't know what to do with it. I slid it against my tender veins but nothing happened.

The phone rang. I jumped and dropped the razor.

What was I thinking?! I answered the phone; it was Mom. I cried tears of thanksgiving to God for rescuing me. He had Mom call me at just the right moment to stop me from doing something stupid. I never tried cutting again, though the pain still seared me and the poems still flowed like the garish blood of red with which I rhymed *dead, bled, crying in my bed*. I never told anyone what happened. I had no one to tell.

I also kept losing weight. How much, I never knew. I just knew I was skinnier than ever, thanks to the steady stream of comments growing slightly less complimentary. Months or maybe just weeks later – time moves slowly in eighth grade – Heather, Leah, and I reconciled. I stayed friends with Amy and Audrey, but I was back at the stoner table with my two old best friends, like nothing had ever passed between us.

Heather was the first person to notice.

"You never eat lunch," she stated matter-of-factly.

"'Course I do," I replied.

"No, you don't. You need to eat something. Here, eat my French fries." To prove I did eat, I ate a fry.

"I just forget my lunch money," I told her.

She gave me a suspicious look but dropped the subject.

The bell rang, and everyone stood to return their trays. I stood up with them. My head felt light. I tried to regain composure but collapsed onto the floor. Everything was swirling, blackening around the edges. I held onto a cafeteria seat for steadiness. Blue and silver specks twinkled before my eyes.

I came around quickly, but Heather had seen enough. She marched me straight to the school office, in spite of my protests and insistence I was fine.

I wasn't fine, and I knew it. I protested, but deep inside I was glad someone had finally noticed. No one had noticed before. Almost a whole school year had passed, and no one noticed. I was invisible. I was skinny, but no one saw why. As soon as that realization met my consciousness though, I plunged it back into the ugly quagmire of denial where I kept all my shameful feelings. *What an awful thought, of course that isn't why I'm doing this! I just like being skinny.*

Heather told the receptionist that I had just passed out at lunch and that I hadn't been eating. It wasn't entirely true; I hadn't completely passed out, but I appreciated the drama that followed. The school nurse rushed out. She thanked Heather and ushered me to her station. She cosseted me, testing my blood pressure, taking my temperature, making me eat a candy bar. The school called my mother to take me home.

In the car, my mom was silent. I was silent too. I wanted her to be the first to speak, and I wanted her to indulge me. I really wanted to be noticed, by her at least.

"Did you really faint?" she asked.

Even though it was more of a swoon, I said yes. When she said nothing more, I ventured, "I guess I don't really eat ever. I guess maybe I'm kind of anorexic."

"You do too eat," she countered.

You only think I eat. I was upset she didn't believe me and upset she wasn't taking me seriously. We were silent the rest of the ride home.

At school, however, the nurse and guidance counsellor took it very seriously. I was monitored at lunch to see that I ate a healthy portion of food on my tray. I had weekly sessions with the counsellor. My friends were told to keep an eye on me and watch out for vomiting in the bathrooms.

She talked to me in depth about what was going on with me. She said she'd noticed I was losing weight and somewhat suspected this might be going on. She showed me pictures of anorexic women and gave me pamphlets to read. She let me skip two class periods one day to watch a documentary on Karen Carpenter of The Carpenters, who had been anorexic and eventually died from the damage her disorder had done to her body. I never could give a satisfactory answer, at least not satisfactory to myself, of why I'd done it. When she asked if I thought I was fat, I said no. I said I was knew I was skinny, but I liked it and I liked getting skinnier. She asked if I had an aversion to food. Not really, I actually liked to eat.

I did start eating after that. After all, I didn't have any real issue with food, and I didn't think I was fat, though as I felt my clothes get tighter, I wanted to run back to my old ways. I didn't want to put on any pounds, but it was a relief to eat again. Eighth grade wound down, and summer came. I was back to a safer weight, so the school checked me off as *Normal* and sent me on my way to enter high school, and all was forgotten.

---

*Though this ceased being an issue for many years, struggles with food and the temptation to turn to starvation and/or purging to distract me from depression resurfaced in adulthood and persist to this day.

Chapter 4
For the Love of Church

> **Stained Glass**
> *I gaze through warbled glass*
> *stained with colors like water*
> *pouring through a faucet*
> *from rusty green pipes.*
> *Light scatters to the floor in shards*
> *bursting through the glass,*
> *and paints the carpet with stories.*
> *Inside the fractured blobs of color*
> *I become Mary of Bethany*
> *washing the glass feet of Jesus;*
> *or, two steps later, the Holy Virgin.*
> *The fragments pass over me*
> *window to window and when I am gone*
> *settle back into their momentary*
> *and sacrosanct canvas of the floor.*

I ALWAYS LOVED GOING TO church. Even as an adolescent, when most of my peers were groaning about having to wake up early on one of their only two days off a week, I looked forward to Sundays more than any other day of the week. We never attended a church where we needed to dress up, but I still enjoyed dressing a little nicer on Sunday mornings and attending both Sunday school and "big church." I loved singing the songs, I loved hearing the prayer requests, I loved when a man or a woman with a stunning voice sang a beautiful solo, and I loved listening to hour long sermons. The church I grew up in had a lead pastor, but the elders often took turns preaching too. I had my favorites: Mr. Ehrhard, the pastor, whose sermons were always challenging and deep, yet understandable, Mr. Dennis who told great jokes, and sometimes Mr. Haigh because his were different and interesting. I had my lesser favorites: Mr. Elliff who always preached about hell, and my dad, who told embarrassing family stories on us. Once, he used me as an example: "Lori has always wanted a red Ferrari, but that doesn't mean she is going to get one. God doesn't always give us what we want, he gives us what we need." I was humiliated, because I had never asked for or even insinuated wanting anything of the sort. I could appreciate that he was probably a good preacher, and I was definitely impressed by his vast knowledge of the Bible, but I resented all the nudges and winks afterwards about someday getting that Ferrari if I work hard enough and save up.

I was good at memorizing Scripture and could beat anyone in a "sword drill". Sword drills were a competition to see who could locate and read a verse from the Bible the quickest. Everyone sat on the edge of their seats, with Bibles clamped shut, waiting for the verse to be called out. "Ezekiel 6:6...Go!" The first person to locate the verse, stand up, and read it was the winner. I knew the order of the books of the Bible by heart and where they were roughly located in my closed Bible. I was awesome at it.

I loved Sunday school as a teenager, though by that age it was more fashionably known as Youth Group. I especially liked when our teachers would do a series on practical matters of living as a Christian teenager. Drugs, sex, gossip, alcohol, these were things that affected me and fit into the context of my life. By high school, I knew all the Bible stories and was ready to figure out how all these stories applied to my daily life. I went to Sunday and Wednesday night Youth Groups. There, we sang modern Praise and Worship songs, prayed, played ridiculous Youth Group-sanctioned party games and listened to talks, usually topical and applicable to our teen lives. Youth Group was a place I felt I belonged... sort of.

At least I should've felt I belonged there. Unlike at school, where even the Christians thought I was too prude or scrupulous, at church a lot of us were serious about our faith. Yet, a majority of the kids at church still went to private Christian schools together where they saw each other every day. I was only a Sunday and Wednesday friend. Most of the time I felt pretty at home with them, but I always knew I was slightly on the outside of their cliques. I tried not to let it bother me.

The only people from church I felt really close to were Zeke, my former fifth grade boyfriend, and Jacob. Zeke and I had always gone to the same church, and in tenth grade, we started dating seriously. By the beginning of tenth grade, I had finally eased out of the stoner crowd at school and come into my own with the more like-minded kids in the AP program, kids who cared less about popularity and more about academics. The Gifted & Talented kids often went on to join the Forensics squad in high school, a competitive acting and debate club. I had joined Forensics in ninth grade and by the end of the year was one of the gang.

Being a part of Forensics had done wonders for my self-esteem and confidence. The students were very diverse, from churchy kids to gay kids to nerds. We were misfits who fit in with each other. For the first time in my life, I actually felt like I had real friends and a true sense of belonging. Even though we all fought like cats and dogs and swapped best friends like Pokémon cards, we were a family, and no one from the outside was allowed to hurt us.

Zeke, though he went to Christian school and had no theatrical affiliations, fit in great with my new friends too. For a year, we were very serious about each other and were certain we would get married after college. When we broke up just before junior year, I was crushed. Thankfully we stayed close friends, because he and Jacob were the two closest church friends I had. With them, I never felt reserved like I did with the rest of the youth group. With them, I could be totally, prudishly, weirdishly me.

But things began to change with Zeke and Jacob. They had started smoking pot. I was always really uncomfortable with this. I talked to them often about how it was unsafe, a gateway drug, all the rest, and they constantly insisted that it was no big deal. By senior year, they were begging me to try it. I resisted for months. Finally one day they talked me into it. I'd been around them so many times while they were high, and they did seem to be having a lot of fun, and it did seem fairly harmless. I tried it. Nothing happened. It was such a let down! I felt I had compromised my beliefs so greatly as to do drugs and yet got nothing out of it. So I tried again. After all, if I was going to sin, I ought to at least enjoy it!

Enjoy it I did. So much so that I started smoking pot regularly with them. I was troubled only by the illegality of the hobby. As three church kids, we spent a lot of time debating the morality and spiritual consequences of smoking marijuana. I spent a majority of my senior year smoking pot with Zeke and Jacob, and their extended group of Christian school friends.

I still loved church and still considered myself a Christian, so the old concern started plaguing me again: Was I really saved? Could someone willingly sin and still be saved? Maybe I wasn't a Christian at all. Maybe Pam had been right all those years ago.

Zeke, Jacob, and I discussed this often too. Jacob particularly felt confident in his salvation, and in mine, certain that our church's doctrine that we could not lose our salvation was true. He believed that marijuana was only a big deal because it was illegal, not because it was inherently wrong. Zeke was less concerned with the matter. I knew I still believed in Jesus as my personal Savior, and I knew I still loved God, but was that enough? I started searching the Bible for answers. It seemed so confusing; on the one hand, it said all I needed to do was believe, which I did, but on the other hand, it said faith without works was dead (*James 2:17*)[1]. Despite my works that backed up my faith – my otherwise Christ-like lifestyle, my sharing the gospel with non-believers, my mission trips, my prayer and Bible study, my kindness and generosity – this one bad work quite possibly cancelled out all the rest. I didn't drink, I didn't have sex, but I was a pot-head, a law-breaker, and therefore unworthy to carry the name of Jesus.

Chapter 5
Raving and Rolling

I GRADUATED HIGH SCHOOL WITH honors. I was set for college. The summer after graduation was exciting and carefree. Zeke, Jacob, and I started going to raves, and the boys started taking ecstasy and acid. I still smoked with them but refused to try anything riskier. At raves, I remained completely drug-free – downers like pot weren't exactly suitable for the rave scene.

At these all night parties, we danced to techno music until we could dance no more. We drank bottles of water to stay hydrated. I really enjoyed the thrill of dancing all night, not coming home until six in the morning, enjoying my pre-college freedom. The guys insisted that I was missing out by not taking ecstasy, though I still didn't see the need. I enjoyed dancing without it.

They wouldn't let up though. The night before I moved to Northwest Arkansas to start college, we all went out with friends to my last summer rave. I was excited and nervous, nostalgic and daring, and I agreed I would try X with them just this one time, as a farewell. I'd seen them rolling, the term used to describe the high one gets from dropping ecstasy, numerous times and knew what to expect.

I swallowed the pill. I had the night of my life.

Despite the horrendous morning after, trying to drive three and a half hours across the state during a miserable come down, I knew this was my new drug of choice. I also realized I no longer cared so much about my spiritual state of affairs. *I'll worry about that later.*

Like most eighteen year olds, fresh out of high school, away to college and living on their own for the first time, I went wild. I met some people who liked to drink and smoke a little weed, and I joined right in with them. I went to frat parties and got so drunk I could barely make it back home – sometimes I didn't make it home, falling asleep at the frat house in some random guy's bed. I still kept my virginity but only just.

One night was particularly scary. I went to a block party with some new friends. They knew I liked to smoke pot and told me there were a few guys smoking in the back room of one of the houses if I wanted to join them. I joined the back room smokers and took a hit of the joint being passed around. It felt instantly different and disorienting. After a single hit, I felt distant and incoherent. I heard one of the guys say, "Break up that rock." It took all my mental powers to formulate the question, "What are we smoking?" I heard the phrase "laced with opium" and that was it. At some point, I left the room and went outside to join the block party. I felt lost and unable to follow my friends. I tried to zone in on them in the crowd but couldn't keep track. I remember nothing else about the night. I must have been taken home, but I don't even remember waking up the next day.

I was getting a little out of control. My conscience was pricking me. I knew in my heart this wasn't the way I wanted to go, but in spite of that scare, which I had learned a lesson from – never smoke with strangers – I was having fun. The fun only lasted for a little while though. The guilt of drinking, smoking pot, and messing around with guys at frat parties was becoming too much for me. I missed church. I missed my relationship with God. My mom was worried about me. I knew this needed to stop, I just didn't want it to. I'd never had so much fun in my life.

Amanda, a friend from high school, introduced me to some people who all went to the same church. After getting a concerned lecture from my mom about missing church each week, I decided I'd better find some place to go the following morning. I had a phone number for Amanda's friend Josh. I called him up and asked for a lift to church.

The next morning, he met me in his car in front of Reid Hall, my dorm, and we began talking about spirituality and faith. Unexpectedly, I started crying. I confessed that I was on the wrong path but didn't know how to get back. I wanted to follow God but just didn't feel it anymore. I hadn't felt anything in quite a while actually. My theological church background was Calvinist, and I told him I was afraid I wasn't predestined (chosen by God) and therefore had no choice in the matter. Maybe I could never be saved. Maybe I was doomed. He assured me that the very fact I was concerned about it proved that God was working in my heart.

The church we went to that Sunday was unlike anything I'd ever experienced in my conservative churches from home. I was amazed at how everyone at this college campus church seemed so alive spiritually. They sang the songs like they meant it with their whole hearts. I'd never witnessed that before. They sang incredible praise songs I'd never heard before, and the lyrics of a Charlie Hall song hit me hard: everything in our lives comes down to one thing, it said – knowing Jesus.

I knew this was supposed to be what life was all about, but it hadn't been for me, not lately. I knew this was true. I wanted more of this kind of faith.

After church, I met up with Amanda for coffee. I was stringing beads and elastic "kandi" for my next rave, talking through my dilemma. After that service, it was clear to me that I needed to get right with God, but I'd only tried ecstasy once and really wanted to try it again. Why couldn't I do both? What was the real spiritual or moral harm in it?

She said to me, "You can't serve two masters.[2] You need to choose either Jesus or drugs." It was too much to ask for at that precise moment. I was really looking forward to rolling again at this next rave. *After the rave*, I thought. Then I'd get serious about God again. She invited me to The Grove for the Sunday evening service.

I went. It was another college student gathering, very modern and hip. The lights were down low, candles burned on the stage, the band rocked. Everyone was standing, singing, arms raised, eyes closed, truly worshiping God. I didn't have that. I desperately wanted that. Sitting in my chair alone in a sea of standing worshipping people, I put my face in my hands and prayed a simple, foolish prayer, with all the weak fervor of the lost.

God, if you could let me feel like these people feel, if you could give me a feeling better than drugs, I'll follow you and never do another drug again.

In that very moment, incredibly, an amazing, unnatural feeling washed over me, a feeling of pure light starting in my head and pouring down through my arms and torso right down into my feet, euphoric as ecstasy, and I knew it was the Holy Spirit. I soaked in every beautiful, heart-rending, unbelievable moment of it, tears streaming down my face, certain at last that God was real. He answered my prayer. He came into me. I was like a newborn. After all those years of being a Christian, I was finally really *in the light*.

I was never the same. I still went to raves, but I went sober. When people asked me what I was high on, I said, "I'm rolling on Jesus!" I witnessed to everyone. I shared my new experience with anyone who would listen. I was a new creation. I loved my new life. Jesus was everywhere and in everything. I prayed and Jesus answered. I was clothed in the white robes of righteousness, and I never touched drugs again.

For the next decade, whenever my faith was in doubt, I took myself back to that very extraordinary time to remind myself how real God was. While I had prayed the salvific prayer as a ten year old lying on the lime green linoleum floor adjoining my bedroom to the hallway, listening to Carmen late in a summer school-free night, the moment I would recall as the turning point in my life was that evening my freshman year of college when Jesus answered my prayer swiftly and immediately, dousing me in the Holy Spirit's light. The joy of my salvation[3] kept me going and going and going like an Energizer bunny whenever my faith needed fuelled.

Chapter 6
Girl Meets Scotland

Refiner's Fire
In a dark and sullied work shed
lined with feathered wood shelves
and splintered work benches
I am the sharp pointed
red-rusted fire poker
hanging across two dirt-caked nails,
you are the blue blazing fire
scorching my body
to melting point, my rusted
embers drip-glow to the ground.

MY FAITH INSTANTLY BECAME MY life, my sole purpose for living here on earth. I believed that to be a real Christian, one had to face all sorts of personal demons – doubt, sin, inconsistencies in doctrine, the problem of pain, world perspective, and human depravity. I could not conceive of a Christian life mattering without all these deep subjects constantly investigated and evaluated. I took great comfort in theology, which structured all of these issues into a systematic framework that helped me make sense of the insensible. In college, I was surrounded by like-minded people. We were all on fire for God. Our idea of a good time was a pint of Guinness at a bar (once we had turned 21, of course) and a good theological discussion. We spent our free time gathering at each other's apartments for Bible studies, and meeting together for prayer in the autumn leaves under campus trees. I discovered that dishonesty with ourselves was only a tool of Satan to keep us from spiritual growth. I tackled all the lust, jealousy, envy, pride, and every other internal sin lingering in the crevices of my heart with righteous furor. All the outward sins I worked hard to curb too, and with each failure, I fell on my knees in repentance and sorrow, asking for prayer from my prayer partners, begging strength from the Holy Spirit to make me more like Christ.

I made some mistakes along the way; I was far from perfect. One night, I went clubbing with some friends from the dorm. I wore a mini skirt and tall boots, and dirty danced with the guys in the club. It all seemed harmless, until the next day, when I was eating breakfast in the cafeteria and reading my Bible, my morning devos. One of the guys who'd seen me the night before approached me.

"You reading a Bible? You a Christian?" he asked. Piously I responded that yes, I was a Christian.

"Girl, those moves you were doing last night ain't no moves a Christian should be doing. You can't go dancing like that one night and then read your Bible the next." I was deeply convicted and humiliated. I asked Jesus to please forgive me for tarnishing my witness.

I wanted to go back on another mission trip with Teen Missions. I was older now; I would be able to go as a leader. I had loved Pakistan and the Muslim people, but this time I believed the Lord was calling me to India, to see how the Hindus and Buddhists lived, and to get a better understanding of the religious and political divide that had split the country in two. I called up the organization, asking if the team to India still needed leaders. The woman on the phone told me all the team leader positions had been filled except for a team to the state of Arizona and to Scotland. Disappointed, I told her I'd have to pray about that.

I hung up the phone, devastated. *Lord, what is this supposed to mean? I thought I was supposed to go to India, not Arizona or Scotland!* Yet before the prayer was even uttered, I knew God was sending me to Scotland. Why? I did not know. Impulsively I phoned back almost immediately and requested the leadership spot for Scotland.

That summer was one of the hardest of my newly rededicated Christian life. At the end of my freshman year of college, I met Alex at a rave. We fell for each other fast and hard. In only four weeks, I was madly in love with him, even though I knew he wasn't a Christian. I had three weeks between moving out of the dorms and flying out for my mission trip, so I lived with him for those weeks. Our relationship was very physical – a big no-no for Christians – but I was enamored. The sexual aspect of our relationship distressed me, but I didn't want our relationship to end over it. We fit together so well, we made so much sense together, and we had fun together. Leaving him for ten weeks felt like an overly severe punishment for our impure relationship.

We wrote each other letters nearly every day. His constant stream of letters were a sweet solace to me in my homesickness during those first hard weeks at Boot Camp. His letters were funny, sweet, and comforting. I missed him badly.

As a leader I had to arrive at Boot Camp, a microcosm of evangelical austerity, two weeks earlier than the start day to prepare the campsite. We had daily leadership training classes, Bible studies, and prayer time. As the Christian devoutness of my surroundings closed in on me, I couldn't help analyzing my relationship with Alex in a spiritual context. I thought about Alex constantly, but the distance brought me clarity to see the ungodliness of our physical relationship. I was tormented with guilt and confusion. I knew the Bible said not to be "unequally yoked with unbelievers ... for what communion hath light with darkness?" (*2 Corinthians 6:14*)[4]. I definitely knew that the sexual nature of our relationship – though we'd never had sex – was displeasing to the Lord. I loved him so very much, but the bottom line was that he wasn't a Christian, and therefore I knew I couldn't be with him. We were unequally yoked. God was telling me to break up with him. It was also clear to me that the breakup needed to happen immediately.

I felt as though God was slicing through my heart with a hundred razor blades. I did not want to end this. I loved him, really loved him, but I forced myself to confess I needed to love God more. It was either him or Him. At the airport after Boot Camp, where we prepared to fly to Scotland for the remainder of the summer, I called him on a pay phone and broke both of our hearts. I then curled up in a dark corner and sobbed. I was making the right choice for Jesus, but the wrong choice for love.

I arrived in Scotland to another sweet love letter, written and sent by Alex several weeks earlier so it would be waiting for me when I arrived. I sneaked away on my own to read it in private with my tears. So many razor blades. God was making this one hurt to ensure I didn't make the same mistake ever again. It was for my own good, I knew that, but it hurt more than I could bear. For the next three years of college, I could not pass by him on campus or in the grocery store without feeling the sting in those old wounds.

I assumed that Scotland, and all of Europe for that matter, was a pretty Christian place. What I discovered when I arrived there was that Scotland, and the United Kingdom as a whole, is very post-Christian. Christianity is fairly outdated and passé there. Our team was an Evangelical team, meaning that instead of hard labor, we were there solely to share the Gospel. We performed street dramas, did puppet shows for children, sang as a choir, shared our testimonies in churches, and ran a summer Bible club in one of the "schemes" (economically deprived neighborhoods). We also spent a little time with a local Christian drug rehab in the area where we stayed. It was all starting to make sense to me why God would send me to Scotland, besides telling me to end things with Alex.

During that first year of college, Zeke and Jacob had gotten more involved with drugs than ever before. Aside from acid, ecstasy and marijuana, they were smoking crack and meth, and experimenting a little with all kinds of other illegal substances. I hadn't touched drugs in almost a year but was still close friends with these two guys. Being involved with this drug rehab center brought it all together. I was able to share my own small experience with drugs with the boys in the rehab, and we felt like there was some common ground. Not many of the kids on our mission trip had any experience with drugs; I began to wonder if maybe God was going to use my understanding of the drug culture to reach drug addicts in the future. Perhaps that is also why I had to break up with Alex. God wanted to use me for bigger things, and he needed me to be all his. Like Abraham being asked to sacrifice his son Isaac in the book of Genesis, I'd been asked to sacrifice Alex. Only God didn't offer me a ram instead.

Or did he?

For that summer, unbeknownst to me, I met my future husband.

I started my sophomore year of college. I now had two possible callings for my life; I was either going to work with drug addicts or I was going to be a missionary to a Muslim country. I started taking Arabic classes. I focused on my relationship with God. My college church had become very focused on Muslim outreach, and this fit in perfectly with my new possible calling. God was bringing everything together. It was all starting to make perfect sense.

I met Dylan. On paper, Dylan was perfect for me. He was a Christian, we went to the same church, he had a great family, and he was an incredible musician. We started dating, and it seemed obvious to me he was "The One" – except our relationship was extremely rocky, full of conflict. We broke up and got back together several times. After my last whirlwind relationship with Alex, I was ready to settle down with someone I could be equally yoked with. However, we were far from equally yoked. Above all else, his life's calling was music, not the mission field or drug addicts, and his feelings for me never matched the intensity of mine for him. I filled journal after journal delineating and analyzing my feelings for him and scribbled long, emotional prayers pleading with God to give me a sign that we were meant to be together, and to give one to Dylan too. I wanted so badly for us to work out that I couldn't see what was right in front of me – we were not right for each other. After a year of back and forth, and a decision to get married, he finally broke it off for good. Once again, I found myself once again weeping in the dark, wondering what God was punishing me for this time, for this relationship was all above board, pure and pleasing to him. Then in the stillness and blackness of the night, balled up in my bed with blankets hugged tightly around my shoulders, I heard God's still small voice say *I saved you from marrying the wrong man.*

I decided to "kiss dating goodbye" (a phrase coined from the popular book by Joshua Harris). Maybe like the Apostle Paul, I was called to be single, so I could better serve Christ. Boys, relationships – these things were just distractions getting in the way of my purpose.

At the end of my third year of college, I travelled back to the UK to do some mission work with Teen Challenge, a Christian drug rehab, in Wales. I asked for prayer at church the Sunday before I left and specifically requested that everyone pray I wouldn't allow my boy-craziness to interfere with God's work and that I would not meet a guy. I was fairly sure I'd received a revelation from the Lord that I was to remain single, if not forever, at least for a very long time.

To my annoyance, I found myself immediately attracted to Scott. I knew Scott from two years earlier, but we hadn't really been friends. As soon as I realized I was attracted to him, I prayed against it. I emailed my prayer partner back home asking for prayer. She asked me if God had really told me not to date anymore or if I was just trying to protect myself after my still recent breakup. I didn't know.

Scott was an unlikely match for me. While he did fit the Christian, Calvinist, and musician categories (I do like musicians), he wasn't who I expected to fall for; he wasn't the outgoing life-of-the-party kind of guy I was used to dating. He was quiet, serious, and introverted. I kept my distance emotionally. Again I felt like Abraham being asked to sacrifice Isaac. We took things very slowly. I liked him a lot, but I wasn't sure if God was giving me this or if I was taking it. I wanted to be sure this was right, so I prayed. Continuously. I sought advice from Kathy, my trusted adult mentor at church about him. (When she later met him, she loved him.) We maintained a relationship long distance for six months. We spoke on the phone for at least an hour every day, and our conversations were very honest and open. In this way we came to know each other really well. My one reservation was his sometimes faltering faith, which made me a slightly uneasy. He had been an atheist a few years before but had returned to the faith he had been raised in. He still had doubts, but he loved Jesus. I had my doubts about the strength of his spirituality, but not about him. I prayed constantly for confirmation from God that this was his plan for us. I knew this relationship was unlike any I'd been in before; it felt rational, peaceful, natural, and unhurried. Our future plans aligned – his church was directly involved with the drug rehab ministry and he was often involved himself – and our relationship was pure, always aiming to keep Christ the center. Our feelings for each other were mutual and equally balanced. I felt he accepted me completely for who I was. I no longer felt I needed a direct sign from God; the peace he had placed in my heart was convincing enough.

When my dad gave his stamp of approval, I was pretty much certain.

He flew out to visit me in Arkansas at Christmas time and told me for the first time that he loved me and that he wanted to marry me. It was quick after that. I graduated from the University of Arkansas with an Honors English degree in August, and we were married in September. After a two-week honeymoon, which included a whirlwind trip to Los Angeles for my immigration interview and visa, I packed exactly three suitcases and moved to Scotland to start my new life with Scott. We'd spent a total of seven weeks together in person before our wedding day.

Chapter 7
How I Started Wearing Hats

SCOTT, LIKE ME, HAD BEEN brought up in church. While I'd been a part of several churches and denominations growing up, Scott had been a part of the same Brethren church his whole life. I became a member of the Brethren when I moved to Scotland after our wedding. The Brethren are an ultraconservative denomination of Christianity, espousing a myriad of old fashioned doctrines that Scott and I disagreed with, including the requirement that women wear head coverings and remain totally silent in church. They have assemblies all over the United Kingdom (and several sprinkled around the world). Scott's church was a part of the Closed Brethren, as opposed to the Open, meaning they believed in near total exclusivity- and therefore members are technically not allowed to attend any other church. While they accept that other churches may be right in some matters, they believe those are not *the* Church of God. Despite my reservations and strong doctrinal opposition, however, I chose to officially join the Church, because I felt passionately about taking the Lord's Supper, and only official members are allowed to partake in the "breaking of the bread" in the Closed Brethren.

The Lord's Supper, more widely known as the Eucharist or Communion, is the practice of believers coming together and taking wine and bread, to remember Jesus' death on the cross. In the New Testament, the Gospels tell of the Passover meal before Jesus' arrest and subsequent crucifixion, where Jesus passed around a loaf of bread and a cup of wine, likening them to his body and blood, and instructed his disciples to "do this in remembrance of me".[5] It has been a fundamental tradition of the Christian Church ever since.

In this church, only members are allowed to take part in the receiving of the bread and the wine; therefore I joined. Not only was "Do this in remembrance of me" a command from Jesus, it was a practice that kept me focused on Christ and kept me humble and thankful for God's grace. Communion had only been taken quarterly in any other church I'd ever attended. Taking the elements every week was special to me; it was at the Lord's Table that I felt closest to him, felt his grace and peace wash over me, despite my unworthiness. So I put on a hat, closed my mouth, and joined, controversial doctrines and all.

That first year in Scotland was rough for me. I'd left my family, my friends, my church, my job, and everything I knew to go live in an unfamiliar city in an unfamiliar country full of strangers with a caustic sense of humor that bruised my American sensitivities. With Scott at work all day, I was isolated in our home atop the hill, overlooking the Clyde and the entire town of Greenock, by a tangled mass of confusing roads I couldn't have driven, even if I had known how to drive a manual shift on the opposite side of the road. Scott was my only sense of familiarity. I tried to carve out a place for myself in our new church but found that just having been one of the Americans who visited with TMI and then subsequently marrying one of their own did not automatically grant me a place in their inner circle. I joined the worship team with Scott and a few of the other young people in the church for Sunday night praise services but spent the rest of my days alone at home, waiting for Scott to get off work.

Getting a job helped fill my empty hours and introduced me to some new people. A few tensions within the church were brewing, and Scott and I grew very uncomfortable with remaining in that particular assembly, so we moved to the Brethren assembly closer to our home. We immediately fell into place there. Our first Sunday there, we were invited out to lunch by several of the young married couples in the church. I swiftly became friends with a few in particular. Once a year had gone by, I had a job, I had some friends, and I knew how to drive a manual. Finding a church home put the final important pieces into place.

From childhood, I had always been vexed over the condition of my soul. What sins were contaminating my life and what earthly idols could be separating me from my Father in Heaven? I was a fallen creature, I believed, constantly sinning and making mistakes, or allowing pride to creep in when my act seemed clean. I assumed every Christian dug as deeply into their souls as I did to root out evil. I'd been surrounded by people like this in my church at college. I couldn't see how one could be a Christian and do anything less.

After I married Scott and moved to Scotland, I discovered this was not the case with everyone. In fact, it seemed most Christians did not scrutinize and analyze their every move and motive, and they did not scour the Scriptures for complete contextual and critical understanding. With the exception of an American couple we met on a Christian internet forum, we knew very few people who were as invested as we were (or at least I was) in immersing themselves so completely in a life lived for Jesus. While Scott and I would spend hours, full weekends even, with this couple, Jonathan and Sarah, discussing systematic theology, cessationism, and paedobaptism together in their little flat in Edinburgh, very few others I met in Scotland seemed all that concerned with the finer points of understanding the Christian faith, or with clearing away the thin, unnoticeable cobwebs of sin in the hidden most corners of their souls. My own husband, a good, intelligent Christian, who was very concerned with scriptural accuracy and theological soundness, did not otherwise seem to share my tendency towards over-analysis and intense introspection. Yet I could be no other way. My whole purpose here on earth was to glorify God. It is the chief end of man; how could I ignore my chief end? How could I live carefree when my heart was so blackened with sin?

Jonathan coined this "spiritual masochism". He too once thought everyone was like he and I, always seeking out the unrighteous in oneself, trying to become more pure and blameless, more like Jesus, in every possible way. It was constant spiritual flagellation; scraping out the insides of our depravity like a cantaloupe, pulling out the seeds, searching into deep and tender places in the quest for holiness. I had a good grasp of forgiveness and grace, and I lapped it up thirstily like a parched animal, but I also had a deep, uncomfortable sense of my iniquity. I acknowledged how sinful I was, then praised the Lord for pouring out his never-ending mercy on a wretch like me.

After about a year in the small town assembly, as much as we loved the people in the church, Scott and I decided we needed to find a church that more closely lined up with our doctrinal beliefs and provided us with more scripturally challenging teachings. We still didn't align at all with much of the church doctrine, and I felt stifled with the ultra-conservativism and the prohibitions on women. We visited an Anglican church in Glasgow and fell in love with it. They were Reformed, liturgical, and totally hipster.

We spoke to the rector about our interest in joining his church. His response was, "We would love to have you as members of our church, but I must first ask you this – is it God who wants you to leave your current church, or is it you? Because if God hasn't told you to leave, I can't recommend you leave. Perhaps God has something in mind for you in that little dying-out assembly?" We thought very seriously about that little piece of wisdom. We acknowledged that it was never God telling us to move, just our own desires. For that reason, we decided to stay in our little Closed Brethren church with outdated practices and doctrines, and we recommitted to making it our church home. I resolved to wear my head covered without complaining for as long as God asked me to.

After all, I really loved the people. They loved me too. I felt very welcomed and included. I made friends with the other young women in the church, and many of the older folks too, and got very involved. My hat collection grew very chic. I stayed because God never told us to leave, and because I felt God had me there for a reason.

Chapter 8
Til Divorce Do Us Part

To My Husband
Don't lose that drip of daylight
I dropped on you that day
when we first played in the green
and ate turnips and peas
at your mum's walnut table.

Don't run when the clouds come
but grab a raincoat and me
'til the sweet orange sun
drips daylight again.

MY FAITH AND COMMITMENT TO Christ was strong, but after a couple of years and the birth of our first child, my husband's started shaking again. I'd become used to that; doubt was the thorn in his side. It was something I'd kind of known deep down when I married him, and it was something I had lived with ever since. In the Christian circles I maintained in college, finding a man who would be a "spiritual leader" was always emphasized as supremely important. We women were encouraged to find a man who would lead us daily in Scripture reading, pray over us unceasingly, and lead us to make Christ-centered decisions. The man was the head of the household, and while we were supposed to be equal partners in the marriage, his ultimate decisions would always be final. We had to be able to trust our future husbands to be the kind of men who followed Jesus selflessly so we could trust their decisions for our families. I trusted Scott's love for Jesus and his sharp knowledge of the Bible but doubted his ability to actively lead.

I had been a little troubled over Scott's lacking in the area of spiritual leadership. When we were dating – if you can call a year of phone calls and emails dating – it was only me who would ever think to suggest we pray together over the phone. I saw young husbands in my hip college church praying fervently over their wives, tears collecting around their bearded chins. I saw the young single men imploring Jesus to save them from their vices, running earnest fingers through their mussed-up hair as they inwardly wrestled with their sinful natures. I saw men prophesying and speaking in tongues and dancing and crying, and I became vaguely aware that my fiancé was not that kind of guy. Scott was reserved, secluded. He'd shared with me his sometimes faltering faith, and I worried a little about it. I knew a woman from church whose husband was a Christian when they married but who fell away for over ten years before coming back. I told my soon-to-be husband I was afraid this would be him one day. He assured me then that it wouldn't. On the other hand, there was my mentor Kathy, who like me was outgoing and sociable and married to a soft-spoken, gentle man. God had shown me, *that can be you*. I decided that our situation would just have to be a little different than all the others. Maybe God had brought us together for me to be the spiritual leader. It didn't seem to quite fit the Biblical model, but we are a fallen race, I reminded myself, and in this fallen world, all is not perfect. Perhaps in time, he would be the spiritual leader God meant for him to be.

But the first couple of years of marriage ended in very little leadership progression. I was still the instigator of family Scripture reading together and prayers. In our Sunday morning Remembrance services at church, men were expected to stand one at a time during the hour long quiet reflection time and pray aloud or give out a hymn to lead the assembly in. They were expected to contemplate and prepare for this all week and give out the prayer or hymn that God had lain on his heart. Scott never did that. He rarely stood to call out a hymn, and he never prayed. He said he didn't feel comfortable praying out loud or calling out hymns, but I couldn't understand why he could easily sing in front of a crowd behind his guitar and a microphone but not choose a hymn to sing during the Remembrance. I quelled the resentment that threatened to grow inside of me towards him.

Then only a couple years into our marriage, he admitted – or rather I forced it out of him – that his doubts had become overwhelming. He didn't think he believed any of it anymore.

The first time he admitted it to me, I was outraged. I knew it! I knew he was never going to be the spiritual leader I should've married! I had prayed for him constantly; I read books about the power of prayer and how to pray for your husband. I seethed that he didn't pray for me like that or read those books. I began attending church alone with our baby daughter, humiliated over our family's spiritual troubles, making up excuses for why Scott wasn't there to save face – though whose face I was trying to save was unclear.

A little while later, he started to believe again, or at least a little more than before, and he came back to church. That's when we started leading worship together in the new more casual Sunday afternoon service, which allowed us ladies to remove our hats and share a few inspirational thoughts from the stage. The Brethren doctrines regarding women had over the past couple of years worn me out. I was used to being very involved in church, but here I felt like women were meant to be seen but not heard. I felt repressed, which led to feeling very disconnected from the church and from God. The idea of raising my daughter in this kind of patriarchal environment really bothered me, so the introduction of this new "family service" was exactly what I needed. Leading worship with my revived husband was beautiful. Two people bonded by vows and made one in the Lord leading the congregation in singing praises to our Savior.

I realized through this new service how hungry I'd been to use my spiritual gifts again – singing, leading worship and sharing the lessons the Lord had been teaching me. I had struggled for so long with wondering why God would grant me so many gifts but not permit me to use them. As a woman, I could not lead a worship service or preach, yet God was constantly revealing truths to me through Scripture that I was certain would bless our little church, if only I were allowed to share them. Now, with Scott back in church and taking the head worship leader position, and the new rules-relaxed family service, my faith was flourishing again. The family service was a huge step in the right direction. I still grappled uncomfortably with the official doctrines of the church on a myriad of issues, but I was at least thankful I could finally have a voice. Scott and I led the worship every Sunday, and I quite often facilitated the prayer request time and gave short five minute talks before the actual sermon on what God was doing in my life or the ways in which he was speaking to me. After all those years of sticking with it, we were finally discovering the reason God had us stay in that little old fashioned church.

Scott still from time to time confided in me his lingering doubts, but for the most part, we had settled into a working spiritually healthy relationship. I was convinced that God would always keep Scott coming back to him – Perseverance of the Saints, we Calvinists called it. God does not abandon his children. Once we are his, we are always his, I truly believed this now. Our marriage would only get stronger, as long as we fought to keep Jesus in the center.

Our second daughter was born. One night, while lounging on the couch with her in a sleep-deprived daze, I got a call that changed my life.

My parents had been married for thirty-two years. Their relationship was solid. They were affectionate with each other and always seemed happily in love. I can recall only a few instances in my childhood of seeing or hearing them fight. They were both devout Christians who believed in the sanctity of marriage. They never joked about or talked about divorce; it was one of their hard and fast rules. They shared this rule with me when I got married. "Divorce is not an option" was their mantra, and it became ours too.

Imagine my surprise when my mom called me to tell me she was leaving my dad.

It made no sense. It just couldn't be. They were Christians; their marriage was held together by Christ. It was the glue that made marriages work, so where was the Lord now? Had my parents fallen so far from his grace that he let them go their own way? Why wasn't he intervening? Was my mother so sinful that she could turn her back on God enough to divorce my dad? I couldn't believe that about my loving, honest mama, but I also couldn't believe that God was going to simply let her walk away from doing what was right.

Marriages can only work with Jesus in the center. (Marriages that work without Christ are just lucky.) Yet as far as I knew, Jesus had been the center for them. Maybe I was naïve, maybe all those years I'd been mistaken, but I was sure my parents' commitment to God was real, so how their marriage could fail was beyond me. I'd staked my own marriage on the belief that as long as we both kept Christ in the center of our lives, he would bless our union. Furthermore, the fact that my parents' marriage was a success had long been the foundation for *my* marriage and its success. It was the proof that marriage works, that people can stay together for life. If my parents can make it, so can we.

Yet they didn't make it.

I was dumbfounded. I felt like the floor had bottomed out from under me. I'd known lots of parents who'd separated or divorced, but I never, never could have believed mine would. I was in total denial over it. I insisted they try marriage counselling. I demanded the full story. I couldn't bear the thought that they were going to divorce. To humor us, my parents attempted one session of counselling, but it was simply too late. My mom had made her decision; she'd been waiting to make this decision for a very long time. It was going to happen, whether I liked it or not.

I couldn't talk about their divorce with anyone. No one would understand. People get divorced all the time; no one would understand what a big deal it was that *my* parents were splitting up. I was an adult but unable to handle my parents' divorce any better than a child.

The effect it had on my own marriage was significant. I looked at my relationship with Scott and suddenly saw nothing but bleakness, an empty sheet of notebook paper with pencil lines drawn and erased so many times that the sheet tore. I saw years of struggling to make it work, years of heartache culminating in nothing but an inevitable, bitter divorce. I gave up. If my parents couldn't make it, no one could. I wrapped myself up in a wool blanket of self-preservation, and locked myself in a soundproof glass room. As far as I could see it, we would never be able to make it work. I closed my eyes and blocked Scott out.

I became frustrated once more with church. The family service was a much needed breath of fresh air, but the sermons seemed so shallow and glib and with everything falling apart around me, I desperately needed substance. I needed theological depth and life-applicable truth. Jonathan and Sarah had long since moved back to America leaving me and Scott no one with whom we could deliberate the deeper spiritual and scriptural concerns of our lives.

Scott and I requested on several occasions that the leadership implement some kind structure to the messages, such as studying a book of the Bible over a period of time, or even focusing directly on a specific topic, something we could really sink our teeth into, but this was ignored time and again. I could sense my commitment to living every moment for Christ waning, and I knew I was growing cynical and jaded. The last thing I wanted was to fall away from Jesus, but the lack of challenge or intelligent teaching was leaving me dry. Still my faith in the reality of Jesus never wavered; I had my intellectual doubts, on such topics as a literal seven-day creation for instance, or the idea of Jonah being literally swallowed by a large fish, but those things didn't stop me from truly believing deep down in God's love and Jesus' sacrifice. However, I still needed something more from my church than just light-hearted messages every week to challenge me and keep me going. The "God is Love" message was growing passé and untenable. With our requests repeatedly dismissed, however, as tends to happen, life went on, and I grew complacent.

As a mother of two small children, I found it harder to attend the early morning Remembrance (Lord's Supper) services. When I did attend, I was distracted by my gurgling baby and chattering toddler, and even when Scott or my in-laws would take the children out for me so I could focus on the meeting for once, my head was clouded with all the thoughts of a sleep-deprived mother – what to make for lunch, did I have enough diapers, could we afford new shoes for the kids, when had I last taken a shower? I was assured by other mothers that I was not alone in this. However, I was suffocating under the doctrines of female submission, despite the new relative freedoms in the family service. While I agreed in general that women should not lead the men or "preach", I felt that the gifts God gave me were growing moss under the shade of my silence.

I was losing Scott. I was losing direction. I was losing motivation.
I was losing interest.

Part 2
During

Chapter 1
The Itch

Hide Not Thy Face From Me
Oh, Lord, if you were
a rare Chinese vase
of flowers cerulean and red,
the fragrance of a lover,
I could truly adore you.
If you were a lion,
gold and fierce,
I would not doubt.
I would bow down and obey.
But no—
You're a planet in a book
only the experts know.
You're hidden
by moons and black holes
and my telescope
broke last week.

IT MAY BE DIFFICULT FOR one who has always had lingering doubts or one who has never believed at all to understand that right up until this point, my belief in the resurrected Jesus and in God the Father was 100% genuine, steady, and honest. Though I sometimes entertained doubts, they were never the kind that up-rooted my deepest core beliefs. Though troublesome doctrines sometimes crashed against the tides of reason, they were never strong enough to crush my faith. Though my enthusiasm for praise and my commitment to religious disciplines ebbed and flowed, the seas were never still. It would not be hyperbole to say that my faith was the very essence of me. Despite my intellectual concerns regarding the inerrancy of Scripture or the improbability of the religion I was raised in being the one true religion, I simply couldn't help but believe. Despite my depression, Jesus was still sweet and precious to me. To one who has no frame of reference, the depths to which my faith in Christ ran is likely unfathomable.

It was May 21st, a typical Sunday morning. I woke up to my toddler crawling into bed with me and waking her little sister who still slept next to me. I stumbled through to the kitchen to pour out bowls of Rice Krispies and make a cup of tea for myself. I showered and got dressed for church. I checked Facebook on my phone. It was a typical Sunday morning except for one thing: This was the day hundreds of Americans following the lead of a fundamentalist Christian radio personality Harold Camping were expecting to meet their Savior Jesus Christ in the sky for the predicted Rapture.

I, like so many other Christians around the world, thought this end-times prediction was ludicrous; after all, the Bible clearly states that no one knows the day or time of the Lord's return![6] It so obviously wasn't going to happen the way Camping predicted. Even though I truly felt sorry for the deceived congregation of Harold Camping, I couldn't help but find it humorous. Facebook friends were all posting snarky comments about it, and I updated my own status with a link to an article about them with the comment "Gotta love the crazies!"

A few minutes later, an atheist acquaintance on Facebook replied to my link with the words, "This made me smile….", then updated *his* status to say how funny it was to see people with crazy beliefs mocking other people for their crazy beliefs. I knew he was referring to me, and I was insulted. *How dare he? My beliefs aren't crazy; he's just a mean-spirited militant atheist.* I tried to put his comment out of my mind. *He's not worth your time*, I told myself. Yet his comment irritated me; his words got right under my skin like a mosquito bite I couldn't help but scratch.

I got the girls dressed, and we headed off to church as usual. Yet I couldn't shake the horrible feeling growing inside me. I told myself that it was actually my own guilt that was upsetting me; it was terrible what those people would go through, how wrong of me to mock them on Facebook! That must be what was bothering me about the whole thing: my insensitivity, not his stupid comment.

It was my week to be on family service Prayer Wall duty, so right after leading worship with Scott, I took the microphone off the stand and pulled the giant flip chart onto the stage next to me. I pulled the lid off a Sharpie and started writing up the prayer requests from church members as they passed the handheld mic around, sharing their burdens with their church family. Before we closed in prayer, I added my own prayer request.

"I'd like to just remember all the people in America who have been deceived into believing that the Second Coming is happening today. They are going to need God's comfort and the assurance of His promises to keep them from losing their faith in Him." Heads nodded in agreement; a deep "Amen" from the other side of the room.

After church, I went home for a quick lunch and some down time on the internet before working my part-time shift at the DVD rental shop. To find out more about the story, I searched the web. In my browsing, I came across a blogger who made the point that mainstream Christians aren't much wiser than their Camping counterparts. They too believe Jesus will return, they just don't have a date set on their calendars. This irritated me even more. I scratched that mosquito bite a little harder.

I went into work that afternoon with the itch. In between handing over new DVDs and filing returned ones, my mind churned over these thoughts. I felt an emptiness in the pit of my stomach open up like I'd never felt before. My thoughts were like an earthflow of sand caving in and rushing down from my brain into my gut. Every spare thought became dedicated to scooping up fistfuls of faith which slid swiftly out of my clenched fists the harder I squeezed. I could not focus on anything else. *We aren't any wiser. We just don't have a date set on the calendar.* I couldn't help but agree with his logic. After all, how many generations have passed since Jesus promised his disciples he'd return before the end of their own? I'm no good with math, but I knew there were a lot. Roughly two thousand years' worth anyway. My head throbbed.

I went home that evening feeling nauseated. *I must ignore this doubt. We all have doubts. I myself have had lots of doubts. This is no different. God will see me through.* I pushed the thought as far from my mind as possible. Ignore the doubts, and they will go away. I crawled into bed early that night to sleep away my anxiety.

Yet over the next days and weeks my mind kept turning this thought over and over in spite of my resistance. I went back to the Bible. I read the chapter every way I could think, but there was very little room for misunderstanding. Jesus said plainly that this generation would not pass without the Son of Man's return[7]. I've heard sermons on this my whole life. I've explained this away to many people myself. "This" generation is a metaphor. "A day in our eyes is like a 1000 years in God's." Jesus was referring to something else. His original meaning was lost in translation. I always accepted all those answers. But plain is plain. Jesus was wrong. Or else he was very unnecessarily cryptic. Either way, that generation and many others did pass away, all of them believing they would see the end of days, and yet we're all still waiting to be taken into Glory.

I had been a Christian all my life. I had faced all kinds of doubts and questions. But this time… this time, it was different.

Chapter 2
Jacqui

ONLY A MONTH PREVIOUSLY, I'D faced one of those doubts. I'd been out at the pub with friends one Wednesday night. I came home feeling cheerful, until Scott met me uncomfortably at the door. With a twisted, unusual expression on his face, he said, "Your friend Jacqui ... died."

I just looked at him. I thought he was going to laugh and say just kidding until I realized that isn't something you joke about. I felt dizzy. The room teetered. This must be a dream. I knew it wasn't.

She had been killed in a car accident that evening on her way to visit family in the Highlands. Jacqui and I weren't incredibly close friends, but she was one of the oldest acquaintances I had in Scotland. I met her on that first mission trip to Scotland in 2001. She was only 16 then, wearing a t-shirt that read "My boyfriend fancies you". I thought that t-shirt was funny, and it was our first talking point when we were reunited years later as breastfeeding mums. We shared a great group of mummy-friends. She and I talked about religion often. She was a Roman Catholic, though not a practicing one, and she didn't have a lot of interest in any kind of personal relationship with Jesus, the way I and other evangelicals believed to be critical for salvation. I prayed for her sometimes.

She and I hadn't spoken in a little while. Our last conversation, via text, had been heated and unkind, and I hadn't bothered to contact her since. Now she was gone. I just couldn't believe it.

The next day, I heard that our friends were getting together to mourn our loss. I showed up and silently listened as they all told wonderful and sad stories about Jacqui. I was overcome with regret and shame over the last conversation we'd had, almost three months ago. Three months. I hadn't talked to her in almost three months. And now she was gone. I didn't say much the whole night. I fought to keep the tears trembling at the brim of my eyelids from spilling; there was enough emotion in the room already without me breaking down.

As I was getting ready to leave, one of the girls announced, deliberately but briefly meeting my gaze, "She never liked most of yous anyway" and laughed a strange laugh. I swallowed hard. That text. Three months ago. She died hating me. There would never be a chance to make it right. I managed to get into my car before completely falling to pieces, arms hugging the steering wheel, shoulders shaking.

I stayed in a broken down state for about two weeks; for two weeks the fog just couldn't clear. Sometime after the funeral, after there was some sort of closure, I began to work my way out of the fog, but the pain and sadness and regret over our last words never left. Had she ever forgiven me for my snippy response to her rude text? Was that comment just someone's grief talking?

Would I see her in heaven?

This recurring question distressed me even more than the regret I was feeling. No matter how much I tried to ignore it, this persistent thought troubled me incessantly: *If what I believe about the Bible is true, Jacqui is in hell right now.*

Hell. It tormented me. I could not believe that just because she wasn't a born-again, Evangelical Christian, she was now suffering eternal punishment. Surely not! The criteria for salvation suddenly seemed too narrow. I'd always believed that the road to heaven was narrow, that many who thought they were Christians would in death find themselves facing a Jesus declaring, "Depart from me, I never knew you."[8] The doctrine I'd always believed completely, and even reasoned was justly administered in respect of God's holiness and sovereignty, was now cruel and evil to me; I refused to think on it any more. I just couldn't.

On the Day Jesus Didn't Return, the problem of hell resurfaced along with my new doubts about Christ's return and the infallibility of Scripture. So many Biblical problems to wade through. So many paradigms to shift. I wanted to ignore them, but the little itch had turned into a raging rash that I just scratched and scratched and scratched, no matter hard how I tried to resist the temptation.

I tolerated these private doubts for several weeks. I could not speak of them to anyone. I absolutely could not tell Scott and have his own doubts more confirmed by mine. *If I don't give the problem a name, it will only remain a little problem,* I thought, but I could no longer deny that this was more than just a "little problem". I knew, as much as I hated knowing, that my faith in Jesus Christ was in serious crisis mode.

Any other time I'd had doubts, I recalled that moment of rededication to Christ, the "joy of my salvation". I reminded myself of what Jesus had done for me in that little college church service so many years ago, the pure light of the Holy Spirit's touch, the immediate answer to my plea. That moment had been so real, so undeniable, that it cleared away any superficial doubts I was having, giving me something to believe in again.

Until now.

I tried. I tried to recall that moment like I had so many times before, but the memory had been flattened, like a spider underfoot. Nothing but a few twitches of a mangled leg was all that was left of that once purifying memory. I tried convincing myself in other ways. I remembered all the other more recent times God had worked in my life, like when Scott and I had just gone to one paycheck so I could stay home and care for our firstborn daughter. Money was so tight, and I couldn't afford dishwashing tablets for the dishwasher. I had to buck up, I told myself, and hand wash. No big deal really. It was the sacrifice we agreed to make so we could raise our daughter ourselves and not put her into nursery. But it underlined our financial state with a big black permanent marker, and that's what worried me. Would we be able to survive? I believed God wanted me to stay home with my child. I knew that's what I was supposed to do. Would God provide?

I worried and prayed and needed some assurance that God was going to provide for us. And in the mail the very day I used my last dishwashing tablet, we received a free sample. Of dishwasher tablets. I rejoiced. Not because I had four more loads I could wash automatically before plunging my rubber gloved hands into a sink of soapy dishwater but because God was telling me he would care for all our needs. *Jehovah Jireh*, my Provider. That little message from God was sufficient for me.

At least it was then. These stories used to bolster me up when my faith was wavering. Now, that story sounded stupid. A bloody coincidence. Nope, it was time to make new memories. The old ones could no longer be relied upon. I needed fresh, new God-moments. God was putting me to the test, that much was certain. The fact that I still cared was proof that he was still in my life.

Chapter 3
Til Doubt Do Us Part

SCOTT AND I WERE HITTING a low point, the lowest in our marriage. One rainy afternoon – it's always a rainy afternoon in Scotland – we got into a fight over something now long forgotten. I was so sick of trying to make our relationship work. I could see no happy ending and just wanted all the pain to go away. My parents' divorce still had a profound effect on me, now nearly ten months later. All the struggling, all the silent treatments, all the half-hearted, tearful make-ups, what was the point? It was time to give up. Angrily, I told my husband to just leave and not bother coming back. He left the house with a loud slam of our heavy front door, and I dropped down onto our brown leather sofa at the bay window of our third floor flat, feeling as heavy as that slammed door, and watched his car drive away.

My tears blurred my vision as I silently wept and stared out the window, praying he would come back. I didn't want him to leave, I realized. I needed him. I didn't see how we could ever make it in the long run, but for now, all I wanted in the world was to see that green Skoda drive back down the road and park in front of our flat. I watched each car drive down that busy street, and my heart leapt every time a green car pulled out of a side road. When what felt like hours later – but was probably no longer than ten minutes – his car reverse parked back into the same space he'd left open as if it had been waiting for his return, I vowed to never let anything come between us like that again. I couldn't comprehend how we would make this work forever, but I could imagine us staying together today. And possibly tomorrow. His pale, worn face and red eyes as he stepped back through our front door was the most beautiful, precious face I'd ever seen. We held each other, and I cried.

The confusion and pain of my parents' divorce compounded by these new doubts were tearing me apart. Yet I couldn't talk to anyone. These were my battles to face alone. We continued to lead worship together at church, but I felt spiritually starved. Church was empty. I was in serious need of help but was afraid to share my doubts with the leaders. I was afraid if I shared my doubts with anyone I'd be either "read out" of the church (excommunicated) or asked to stop leading the worship, the one place I still felt close to my Savior. At best, I feared I'd be patronized for the "little doubts we all have"; these were nothing like everyone else's "little doubts". I kept my troubles quiet for the most part and kept going as best I could. I would follow Jesus at all costs, faith or no faith.

Scott always said that playing guitar and singing praise songs were when he felt closest to Jesus. But when I stood next to him in front of the church, I felt like a pair of frauds. We looked like the perfect happy Christian couple, but I didn't know if we would last, I didn't know if he still quite believed anymore, and I wasn't sure if I believed either. I hated feeling false. The spiritual masochist inside was plunging its judgmental finger right through the hole in my heart. I carefully picked the songs we sang; I skipped over songs that stated out right "I believe in Jesus". I couldn't honestly sing some of those words, but I could choose songs that reflected what was truly going on inside my soul, songs that begged for help or stated the desires of my heart. I could still sing those songs with my eyes closed and still mean them.

No one knew a thing. I kept it all inside, yet I knew I needed to talk to someone, and that someone had to be my husband. Finally one night, as we crawled into bed, I garnered up enough courage and verbally tiptoed around the doubts in my head. I tentatively admitted that I wasn't sure if I believed in God or the Bible anymore. He squeezed my hand and was silent.

I needed him to speak. Now, more than ever, I needed him to encourage me. I'd been the spiritual leader for so long, now I needed him to be. I needed him to tell me everything was going to be all right, that God was still there and I was not losing my first love, my center, my All In All. And that I was not losing my husband either.

Silent tears dripped off my temples onto the pillow. I needed him to say something.

He finally whispered coarsely, "I'm sorry."

I stared at the ceiling. *That's all? That's all you can say?*

"Sorry for what?" I asked with a sigh.

"It's all my fault. If it weren't for me, you wouldn't be having these doubts."

Long silence... infinitely long. I couldn't breathe, like I'd been kicked in the back. His words had sucked all the air out of the room. It all hit me at once, finally dawning on me. I'd never understood before, I'd never gotten it, that all those times I silently criticized him for his lack of faith, he was already blaming himself for his inability to be the spiritual leader I so wanted him to be. All the secret blame I'd been placing on him, he'd been heaping on himself too. Now he blamed himself and his lack of spiritual leadership for my faltering faith. Side by side, lying on our backs in the darkness, hand in hand, we silently cursed ourselves for all our perceived wrongs we had done each other. But he wasn't to blame for this. No one was.

We were quiet for a long time. I'm not sure we said much more of anything. I kissed his cheek and rolled over. Admitting it out loud had changed everything.

Chapter 4
Thanks To Theology

I USED TO BE A REGULAR on a Christian online forum called Christian Guitar Resources (CGR). It's where we met Jonathan and Sarah. The forums weren't all about guitar, though there was a large section devoted to guitar playing and sharing tabs for praise music. I joined the forums in college when Scott introduced me to them. Scott was a mod on the Secular Music forum, but I found a home in Theology. I was a budding theologian, and I lived and breathed theology. I had recently become a strict Calvinist, which put to rest my fear of losing my salvation, and this forum was a great place to delve into my new understanding of Scripture.

To describe Calvinism briefly would be impossible, but basically, there are five main points to Calvinism, otherwise known as the Reformed tradition, named after John Calvin, a prominent figure in the Protestant Reformation. It is summed up with the word TULIP. Calvinists believe:

We were born *Totally Depraved* (T), utterly unable to make any good decision leading us to salvation.

Long before this earth was created, God *Unconditionally Elected* (U) those who would be saved, whom he would make his people, based not on anything we would do or be, but on his own free choice and purposes alone.

He sent Jesus to die on the cross, but while this sacrifice was made for all, his blood actually only atoned for and cleansed the elect (those he had chosen before time), in effect being a *Limited Atonement* (L) rather than universal.

God then reveals his *Irresistible Grace* (I) to those people he has already elected and accepted atonement for, so that when the grace of God is revealed to them, they will be so amazed by how wonderful it is, it will be irresistible.

They then begin a life following Jesus as Savior and will continue to *Persevere* (P) for the rest of their earthly lives and will pass into heaven upon physical death. Nothing will stop them from persevering, because just as they were chosen based on nothing they had done themselves, they cannot lose their salvation by anything they do. Some call this *Preservation of the Saints*, rather than *Perseverance of the Saints*, since it is God's preservation of his chosen that really sustain them rather than their own works of perseverance.

I spent hours upon hours debating the finer points of Calvinism and all other matters of theology on the forums. I grew very knowledgeable of Scripture through study and debate and could argue almost any point. Even in person, I enjoyed arguing, or "discussing", theology with anyone willing to talk about it. In the theology forums, many difficult subjects often arose, some of which made me uncomfortable. So sure was I that the Bible offered complete truth though, I did not fear searching it for the answers to these uncomfortable subjects. I came to recognize that one can have intellectual doubts without it destroying one's faith. For all the intellectual doubts of my own that I forced myself to face, I always managed to find a Biblical argument to counter it. Some of them I didn't like, for instance, the concept of an Elect meaning the rest of humanity was essential sentenced to hell by God for not choosing them, but I dared not question God's sovereign will. Eventually, I found a way of embracing even these most difficult doctrines; after all, we are all so inherently wicked, that it is only by God's most incredible mercy that he even allows a single one of us to be saved when we so entirely don't deserve it. In this way, I addressed many of my intellectual doubts and theological concerns, buoyed up by a genuine, deeply held, honest, and inexplicable belief in the existence of God and the truth and inerrancy of his Word. God had to be right, I had to be wrong, and the point of theology was to find a way to Biblically align myself with God's way of thinking in order to glorify him and become more like Christ.

After moving to Scotland, forum discussion slowly became a thing of the past, but I still discussed theology with Scott, Jonathan, and Sarah and any other friends who would tolerate it. All of our get-togethers in that Edinburgh flat involved dark beer, cigars, and theology... just like I imagined the ancient Reformers before us would have done.

With my faith fraying at the edges, I returned to CGR for support. To my surprise, another former regular had recently started a thread on exactly what I was dealing with – not sure he was a Christian anymore, not sure he believed or even cared about it anymore. That was our one difference; I still cared.

The responses – for the most part – were non-judgmental, yet largely unhelpful. Only one poster's remarks stood out to me. He said that faith had three stages:

First, we have faith in God *because of what we see*. This includes evidence in our own lives or the lives of others around us. It includes any sort of "salvific moment" we may have experienced (like my moment on the floor of my bedroom listening to Carmen) and all of those superficial "Jesus found me a parking space" occurrences. We believe in God because we feel him or "see" him.

Second, as this faith matures, it becomes about *what the Bible teaches*. We begin to distinguish that what we feel and what the Bible teaches are often not the same, and we must rely on the Bible only as our foundation for faith.

The third stage is when we go beyond believing in God because of what we feel and beyond believing because the Bible tells us so. This is when we believe solely *because we can't live without it*. In the face of all the evidence stacked against it, in the face of virtually no reason to believe it, we believe any way out of pure, blind faith.

I suspected I was in the third category, and it gave me encouragement. Maybe God was elevating me to this exceptionally hard stage of faith to make me stronger. I realized I believed and loved Jesus not with my head but with my heart because "to whom shall I go?"[9] I decided that I would live on in utter blind foolish faith, like a child, out of obedience to the Lord.

So I was obedient. I continued to lead worship at church. I tried to read my Bible more, attempting to read it straight through, starting with the first book of Genesis, but this was counterproductive. The Old Testament is full of confusing stories of God destroying people and making laws that lowered women and commanded cruelty to men. The more I read the Old Testament, the more I felt the threads of faith being pulled out of the tapestry. I'd read these same words and stories many, many times before without hesitation or difficulty, but now each subjugation of a people group, each law requiring cruel punishments and practices, each unreasonable test God administered on his people to get them to prove their loyalty to him, confounded me. I had to settle with the uncomfortable, and no longer very Calvinistic stance that I simply did not believe everything in the Bible was accurate, literal, and true. I knew it was unorthodox, but it had to be admitted, and it had to be the card I tossed out to keep my faith alive.

Scott felt if one part of the Bible couldn't be relied upon, none of it could. I had to hold onto a different opinion. At the very core, I still believed Jesus was the Son of God and died on the cross for me. Or, at least, if I didn't totally believe it, I still clung to that part for my salvation. It was still the most beautiful and precious part of the Bible to me, that Jesus' robes of righteousness could cover all my unrighteousness. I needed that part. I couldn't live without that part. I knew I could no longer honestly believe a large portion of the Bible as literal anymore, so I made an exchange. I prayed God would allow me that weakness of faith but still grant me the faith to believe in Jesus. I never wanted that weakness to be a lasting one; I prayed fervently that God would one day restore all my faith. Yet for the time being, I needed to focus on the crux – Jesus as my savior.

I prayed often, sometimes constantly. Throughout the day, I maintained my usual flowing conversation with Jesus. I was accustomed to speaking to him regularly, whether thanking him for things, or confessing an inappropriate thought or deed, or asking for strength and help. I continued to share my faith with my young children. We prayed our bedtime prayers together, always ending our long, and ever increasing list of things we were thankful for ("my pink bunny, my sparkly shoes, my banana, my new best friend") with, "And most of all, thank you for Jesus." I prayed that particular last line with utmost sincerity. If nothing else, I was thankful for Jesus.

At night, whenever I could face the heartache that bringing up the subject would trigger, I lay in bed and gave it all to God. Inevitably I'd start with, "God, I don't even know if you are there", followed by a quick apology – "and I'm so sorry about that" – and then I'd begin.

I spoke honestly, bluntly, and agonizingly to God about my doubts, my fears, and my desires. I confessed how utterly desperate I was for him to offer me a little faith again before I lost it all completely. I promised I'd continue living for him no matter how long it took, if he would please just give me back my faith. All I wanted was that faith I'd had before, an honest, sincere belief accompanied with acceptance of that which I found uncomfortable – or even distasteful. I wept miserably. Sometimes my prayers were passionate, exploding from my heart, an offering of complete surrender.

All I felt after each prayer was exhaustion. Sleep was a welcome relief from the anxiety constantly bubbling within me. In all my pleading, I waited for some sense of acknowledgement from God that he was at least listening, that my prayers weren't merely hitting the ceiling. But God had seemed to vanish entirely. It was as if from the very moment I questioned the certainty of Jesus' return, God had pulled down the curtain, snapped closed the shutters, and cut me off completely. He was nowhere. He had disappeared in a puff of smoke. He abandoned me. I felt no comfort, no encouragement, and no still small voice... just silence.

God's silence was oppressive and suffocating, like a heavy, invisible weight on my chest compressing my lungs. I was coming to know too much about God's silence. I'd been withering under the shade of his silence for over a year now, wondering how long it would take for him to break it. That is, if he ever did. I read a book by Shusaku Endo called *Silence*, and what frightened me most about the story was the realization that God may never choose to break the silence, or sometimes he waits until it's too late. I was running out of oxygen. *Oh, God, please don't wait until it's too late!*

Chapter 5
Pascal's Wager Part 1: Blessed Assurance, or How I Stopped Wearing Hats

The Shortest Calvinist Poem Ever Written
I am the last falling petal of the tulip
He loves me, He loves me not.

INTELLECTUALLY, I KNEW I COULD not logically believe in God any more, yet faith was still a spark in my heart. I took that as a sign that God was still there, not letting go of me entirely. *This is just a test of my faith. God is taking me further, to a deeper place I've never known. I will pass this test. I will persevere.*

Still, my mind brought up question after question. For each question, I already had an answer. I imagined a non-believer asking me these questions – how would I respond? I'd been studying God's Word and sharing my faith with people my whole life; there were no new answers to be found. For every question on this miserable test God had assigned for me, I automatically knew how I should answer, but these answers now seemed woefully insufficient. Perhaps they'd been sufficient for me when I had an abiding faith, but now, as a fledgling non-believer, they seemed weak and unconvincing. I could pass this test on paper, but I was failing the practical.

I was convinced that a true believer will hang on until the end, in spite of his doubts and struggles along the way. Yet I also knew of people who were once Christian but later left the faith, essentially proving they were never saved to begin with. (*"They went out from us, but they did not really belong to us. For if they had belonged to us, they would have remained with us; but their going showed that none of them belonged to us." 1 John 2:19*)[10] This thought perplexed me a great deal now. Surely God would keep hold of me, help me persevere to the end! Unless – I was never his to begin with. My biggest fear growing up was being one of those to whom Jesus would say plainly, "Depart from me, for I never knew you." That fear returned. I believed in Jesus, which should have been the only criteria, but now I needed assurance. I needed certainty.

I had for so long been confident and secure in my salvation, not because my life was squeaky clean, but because I trusted God with my life. Now I could do nothing but cling tightly to that security as if it were the rope hanging off the edge of the cliff from which I'd fallen. I could not fathom why God was testing me so brutally, why he was so silent, why he refused to comfort me. All I knew was that there *was* a reason, there had to be a reason, and my perseverance was a sign of my salvation. As I continued going to church, I hoped to one day be blessed and encouraged by something there. As I continued to pray, I hoped one day Jesus would answer me. As I tried to read my Bible more regularly, I hoped one day his Word would speak into my heart.

Once in a while, someone would say something at church that touched me. More often than not, however, church discouraged me. The words spoken from the pulpit often tormented my already weakened spirit, kicking me while I was down. One week the message would be about God's unconditional love and his promise to answer us when we call – *kick* – then another week would be a harsh challenge to spend more time with God, claiming our lack of time with God was the reason behind our doubts – *kick*. Another week someone would share how deeply God touched them that week, speaking directly into their lives just when they needed him most, when they were ready to give up. *Kick.* God loved everyone so much. Everyone but me. Me, he had banished. Me, he kept kicking.

Once in a while, prayer would soothe me. After pouring my heart out to God in bed, my pillow wet with tears, sometimes I felt relief. I felt things might get better. I never felt God had answered my prayers in the way I expected, but I accepted that any small feeling of hope was something, and I could fall asleep a little lighter. Most often, however, praying did nothing but agitate me further. I knew the stories in the Bible. I knew how God often answered prayers in very clear ways – Elijah, when he called down fire from heaven to prove to his idol-worshiping neighbors that his was the One True God, and Gideon who asked for a sign from God twice when his faith was weak, and God graciously granted him his request. I also knew God sometimes did not answer clearly – as in the case of Job. Job had been a righteous man, but God tested him to the limits of his life, taking away everything he had just to prove to Satan that Job would never curse God. If God was testing me this way, I held fast to the hope it was only because he knew I would not curse him, just as he trusted Job.

Once in a while, when I'd open my Bible, praying with my fingertips that God's perfect words for me would be waiting where they touched, God seemed to speak to me through Scripture. One particular time I opened the Bible to the page where Isaiah 62:11 jumped out at me, filling me with hope and thankfulness: "Say to the daughter of Zion, 'Surely your salvation is coming.'"[11]

Of course, I also tried being more systematic about it, by reading the

Gospels straight through, knowing I couldn't rely on chance openings every time. I wanted God's Living Word to breathe oxygen into me once more. But the printed black words on the micro-thin pages that had once pulsed with lifeblood from the very heart of my heavenly Father were now flat and cold, like a corpse. No matter how I prayed as I read, no matter how I tried to hear God speak to me through his Word, I usually came out emptier than when I'd started.

I was pregnant again. At the beginning of this third pregnancy, Scott and I began discussing the possibility of moving away from Scotland back to my home state of Arkansas in America.

Between constant talk of baby plans and moving plans, the lines of communication between us began opening up again. Once I realized all the pressure I'd been putting on him not only to be a better Christian husband, but also to be a better Christian altogether, I eased off. We got back to just talking again, shooting the breeze, and enjoying each other's company.

When topics of conversation got serious, I tried to listen more openly to what he had to say. We talked late into the night about our beliefs and questions and doubts and worries. He began to confide in me the depths of unbelief he had reached. Little did I realize how afraid he'd been to open up to me about his faith; so afraid in fact, that he thought I would leave him because of it. It shamed me to realize he'd been feeling this way. I was finally able to share my doubts more openly with him too. Having someone I trusted to talk to about them, even though the subject was still incredibly painful for me, helped me sort through my emotions.

My pregnancy turned out to be a magical time for us. I was beginning to realize two vastly important things about our marriage: First, that it was not my parents' marriage and had nothing to do with them, nor did it have to follow in their footsteps. Second, we were not doomed to failure just because Jesus was no longer the central part of it. Scott was finally able to question everything safely and even eventually come to reject the beliefs of his upbringing, without the fear of losing me, and so was I, without the fear of our relationship falling to pieces as divine punishment. Our relationship began to flourish again.

I still kept my struggles generally quiet, speaking of them to no one but Scott, afraid of what anyone else would think. My non-Christian friends would see my weakness as proof that God did not exist. My Christian friends would think I was a hypocrite for still leading worship at church. Yet I knew the Bible said to "confess your faults to one another and pray for one another that you may be healed."[12] If I was going to try everything under the sun to get myself right with God again, I had to try even the most painful, most vulnerable routes.

I invited Mandy over after our church's Tuesday morning toddler play group. Mandy and I had known each other through church for years now, and I trusted her. She had been the only person outside my family that I had talked to about my parents' divorce a few years earlier. Our kids were friends, so while they played in the bedroom with the toys, we warmed our hands with a rare cup of still hot tea at my kitchen table. We talked about the usual mum things, and the conversation then naturally turned to church. Mothering and church were the two things we had most in common. I took a deep breath. It was now or never.

"I've ... been really struggling with doubt lately," I began.

I dove right in, explaining how, having been a Christian my whole life, I knew all the "answers" but the answers weren't cutting it anymore. I assured her I knew I was supposed to pray about my doubts, but what good is prayer when you don't even know if you believe in the one to whom you are praying? I knew I was supposed to read my Bible, I told her, but what good is reading a book you aren't sure is even true (and are quite certain is metaphorical and inaccurate)? Mandy listened carefully and compassionately, and to my relief, she did not judge me. She understood my predicament, and far from trying to give me the right answer, she simply listened. She had a cousin who had been in the same situation as me before and had said the same things I was saying. Her cousin later found a church with answers, and her relationship with God was thriving again. This was very encouraging news. *I'm not the only one around here being tested by God, and God is not abandoning us all.* My church had been short on answers for years, and I knew it was definitely time to finally seek out a new church with better answers. First, though, I would have to officially leave the Closed Brethren.

Scott and I had been asking for deeper, more challenging sermons for a while with no success. Then right at this time, right as I was ready to leave, we got some good news: the church was going to do a six-week sermon series during the family service with an additional Sunday evening Bible study to discuss the morning's sermons. The series would be on the end times; not my favorite subject by far, but it was a start. The Brethren doctrine regarding the end times was another that Scott and I disagreed with, but I was nonetheless pleased that the church had finally heard us and were trying something. I resolved to attend the six-week services and even felt a little excited about debating in the evenings with the deacon presenting the series.

The deacon, Graeme, who would be heading up the series, was not the most popular fellow in our church. He was a man in his sixties that was pretty interesting to talk to outside of church but could be a real stickler within, a real by-the-book type who often rubbed people the wrong way, including me. However, he was a nice enough guy, and more importantly, I had become very close to his wife, a gentle, quiet, thoughtful woman who struggled with depression stemming from a childhood raised in a cult. I was always attracted to Mary's selflessness, wisdom, and kindness.

I went along to the first evening meeting following the morning sermon. It was an informal gathering with only a handful of church members around a table drinking tea and eating biscuits. I thoroughly enjoyed the conversation and particularly enjoyed a little sparring match with Graeme over some Bible verses discussing how we will know the end is coming. Afterwards, I thanked Graeme for his time and had a little chat with Mary. Feeling that Mary would understand, I mentioned how great this evening had been for me, because I was struggling a lot with doubt. She listened knowingly and acknowledged her own struggles with doubt and depression. We agreed to meet up that week for a coffee to talk more. And we did.

A week later, I found myself excited about church for the first time in far too long. I dressed myself and the kids for church, put on my red vintage cloche hat with the red rose on the side, and arrived early for the Remembrance - something else I hadn't done in far too long. I felt renewed, refreshed. As the family service began, I noticed quite a few people leaving before it started. During the singing time, which Scott lead alone so I could spend some time praying and worshiping on my own, I saw Mary sneak out of the kitchen in tears, and Graeme chase after her bewildered. He came back in, picked up his suit jacket, put it back down, and picked it back up again. Their daughter whispered animatedly to him then left after her mother. Graeme put his jacket back down and sat back in his seat. He then went forward to give the sermon. I wondered what had happened.

I found out that afternoon at lunch. My father-in-law filled me in on the details; several members of the church were strongly opposed to Graeme giving the messages and were boycotting the sermons. A woman in the kitchen told Mary that she and others were unhappy with her husband leading the messages because no one liked him and the leaders should have chosen someone else. This understandably upset her. Graeme had decided to go ahead with the sermon that morning after his daughter told him she would take care of Mary, but the evening discussion time was cancelled until further notice.

I was outraged.

That was it. Final straw. I sat down that week to draft our resignation letter, which detailed the two main reasons we were leaving: the lack of teaching and this most recent display of un-Christlike love. I was very clear and attempted to keep the letter matter-of-fact, to avoid being labeled "bitter". I mailed the letter to both elders in the church and requested that the letter be shared with the deaconship as well (of which Graeme was a member).

The elders refused to share the letter with the deacons, but that did not stop one of them from bringing it up with Graeme and Mary during a meeting that was supposed to be for reconciliation over the church members' boycott and hurtful behavior towards Mary. However, he did not tell them what was in the letter but simply told Graeme that it was because of *him* that Scott and I had left the church.

I discovered this through my father-in-law who had spoken with Graeme after the meeting. The nerve! I was deeply insulted. Fortunately, by mere chance, my father-in-law, who was hiking buddies with Graeme, had already shown the couple our letter of resignation prior to the meeting, so Graeme was able to refute the accusation right then and there to the elder's face. Still, this did not make me any happier. To think that had he not already seen our letter, he and his wife, *my friend*, would have believed that they were the reason we were leaving. The lies!

And things turned nasty. I confronted the elder about his blatant misrepresentation of my letter, and demanded that the truth be made public. When he refused to set the story straight, or even take any responsibility for his lie, I could take no more; if the letter which the elders refused to share with even the rest of the leadership was going to be misrepresented in hurtful ways, then there was only one thing I could do to ensure it didn't happen again. I published our letter myself on my blog to set the record straight. I would not risk more people being lied to and potentially damaging more relationships.

In response, he read out a statement to the congregation comparing us to "the enemy that came and sowed tares among the wheat, and went on his way"[13]. The enemy in this Biblical passage, by the way, refers to Satan.

There was no question amongst the church members now that Scott and I were "having problems". Many people stood up for us (some even walked out of the building upon hearing the statement), but many were also very unhappy with how I'd chosen to publicize our "dirty laundry". Despite what they may have thought, though, I honestly wasn't bitter towards church in general or towards God. I still desperately wanted to believe, I just needed to find a new place to worship. Though I was weary with Christians and their hypocrisy, my own included, I had promised God I would continue, still hoping he would reward me one day with genuine faith again. Even if by now all the wind had been knocked out of me.

I allowed some time to pass before searching for a new church. I gave birth to my son. I enjoyed sleeping in on Sundays or taking the kids hiking as a family instead. Scott's dad encouraged me often to not let too much time pass before moving on, lest I grow complacent (*grow* complacent?), so soon I was ready to set my Sunday morning alarm again and go church hunting. I knew Scott wasn't interested in finding a new church, so I took the three kids on my own.

Scotland, though it used to be the heart of Presbyterianism, is no longer a religious nation. Churches abound, but many are extremely liberal and do not teach what I believed. Finding a church that fit the criteria I needed was difficult. Yet I wondered if my closed-mindedness was exactly what God was trying to change in me. I sucked in my theological pride and visited a charismatic church, a church as far from Calvinistic as it could be. (I had long ago abandoned the notion of speaking in tongues and prophesying that were so prevalent in my charismatic college church.)

I went with my three children. My daughters went into the Sunday school but my son was only a newborn, and I wasn't ready to put him in a nursery with people I didn't know in a church I'd never visited before. I opted to keep him in the service with me. He was a quiet, non-fussy baby, and I wasn't worried he'd be distracting. I sat towards the back anyway just in case.

A kind elderly woman, approached me before the service began to inform me of the childcare. I politely refused, saying I preferred to keep my baby with me, since he was so young. She smiled and moved on. During the greeting time, another person informed me of the nursery. Again I politely refused. The service continued, and my son was quiet and content.

The prayer time made me uncomfortable; everyone around me murmured their own slightly audible prayers while a few people stood and prayed loudly for all to hear, sometimes in tongues. It seemed to go on forever, but I tried to open my heart. *Is this what you want for me, God?* I asked.

Then the pastor began to speak. Her message was completely irrelevant to me and my struggles, but I wanted to give the church a chance, keep an open mind. I listened from my back pew, pushing away my discomfort with a female preacher, and tried to hear God's voice through her sermon. Then suddenly...

"Excuse me, you do know we have a crèche where you can leave your baby?"

I sat straight up, stunned. I looked around; was she talking to me? Did that really just happen? The pastor from the pulpit was indeed addressing me. She had stopped her sermon and addressed me in front of hundreds of churchgoers. All eyes turned to stare at me and my baby who was silently and discreetly breastfeeding. My face burned crimson. Was I supposed to respond? Out loud? In front of all these strangers?

"I- I'm – It's okay, thank you," I stammered. She smiled an odd smile, as if she'd never seen a mother keep her baby with her during a church service, and continued her sermon. Once I was almost sure the attention was finally off of me, I allowed my humiliation to spill out in silent tears. *How, God, is this helping? Why are you doing this to me?!* I was sure I could feel his mocking laughter rattle the wooden beams of the sanctuary.

I knew I would never come back to this place.

I tried the Church of Scotland, infamous for its wide variety of differing beliefs from parish to parish. I had connections to one particular kirk, so I tried going there. I was friends with the minister and loved his sermons. Though his sermons were never deep or terribly theological, they were practical and I wondered if a little practical, a little "milk"[14], was perhaps what God knew I needed. I felt torn though; I was aware that the minister was gay – though not publicly, since the Church of Scotland had not yet agreed whether ministers could be practicing homosexuals or not. Though I'd long ago accepted that it didn't matter *to me* if someone was gay, I still wasn't sure I how I felt about a church that was okay with it. It was a conflict I couldn't explain. How I could be personally unconcerned with one's sexuality yet still be concerned with a church's acceptance of it made no sense to me. So I overlooked my minister friend's sexual orientation and tried to hear God's voice through him. I heard lots of great life advice, but nothing directly from God. I spoke to him one day briefly about my doubts, and he told me about a time in his life when he too was ready to throw it all away, when depression and doubts nearly destroyed his belief in God. Yet God had returned to him, and he prayed God would return to me.

God returned to him. Would God return to me? I attended that church for a few months but never felt it was home.

I had one last option. A couple of my younger daughter's friends from school attended another Church of Scotland parish church. It was worth a try.

I immediately felt welcome. Rather than giving me strange looks for keeping my son with me in the service, elderly ladies tickled him, the people behind me giggled good-naturedly when he made sounds, and everyone told me what a lovely, well-behaved baby he was. My daughters loved being in Sunday school with their school friends and loved that the minister was also their school's chaplain. I sat with the other mothers and became instant friends with them. Most importantly, the minister's messages were exactly what I'd been looking for. They were contextually sound, Biblically grounded, practical for everyday life, and humbly delivered. Every once in a while I detected a tiny whisper that might have even been God's voice. This was the church I needed. I formally joined the church for the remainder of our months in Scotland and prayed that God would lead me to a similar church home when we moved to America.

My certainty of salvation kept me going. It was Pascal's Wager, in a way. Pascal's Wager states that if you follow Jesus Christ and it turns out not to be true, then you will have lost nothing, but if you do not follow Jesus Christ and it does turn out to be true, you will lose everything. I didn't know if I believed in God or if he was real, but I would continue following him no matter what. It would be worth it in the end should it all turn out to be true. I relaxed in the confidence that my salvation could not be taken away from me, that "neither death, nor life… nor things present, nor things to come… will be able to separate [me] from the love of God"[15] … if it was true. My salvation was not dependent on my faith in God, but in God's promise to me... if it was true. If it turned out not to be true, what would I have lost? I could settle with this.

I had our son dedicated to God in a church service the same way my daughters had been. Similar to a christening, I held my son before the church and publicly stated my intent to raise him in a Christian home and teach him about our Lord. I fully intended our three children be raised up to love Jesus despite my doubts, and Scott supported me in this.

Chapter 6
The Mustard Seed

A FEW MONTHS AFTER MY son's dedication, we moved back to America after having lived in Scotland for nine years. I was determined, eager even, to find a church. I hoped that back in Arkansas, we'd find just the right place to revive our faith. Scott even agreed to come back to church with me. We visited a quaint little Presbyterian church that taught all the right messages theologically but had no children in its congregation. My children were the main reason I was so determined to find a church in the first place, so we kept looking. It was the summer holidays, so I sent my kids to a few different Vacation Bible Schools in the area to help them make friends. One VBS group wanted the kids to do a presentation in the Sunday service after the week was complete, so we went as a family to see our kids perform. It was a Lutheran church; we'd never really considered attending a Lutheran church before. We'd always considered them "practically Catholic".

However, it amazed us. The preacher, Pastor Mac, was exuberant, welcoming and most of all, genuine. The kids loved the church, and my husband and I liked it too. We were pretty sure we'd found our church.

The Lutherans have a not-quite Roman Catholic, not-quite Evangelical approach to Communion (the Eucharist). Evangelicals see Communion as a symbol or a sign, a way of simply remembering Jesus' sacrifice on the cross. That was how I'd taken the Lord's Supper my whole life, and particularly for the past nine years in the Brethren Church. The Roman Catholic doctrine is that the bread and wine are actually physically Jesus' body and blood. Lutherans stand somewhere in the middle, believing that while the elements are not physically Christ's body and blood, the "real presence of Jesus" is with the elements. I was unsure of this stance at first, but the following Sunday when all believers were invited to come to the front of the sanctuary to take Communion together, I timidly stood up and went forward. As I walked down the aisle, I allowed my tears to flow in mascara-rivulets down my cheeks. I realized I hadn't felt this close to Jesus in a very long time. As I took the little piece of bread and tiny cup of wine, I lifted heart-felt praise to the Lord for restoring me with this tiny, ever so tiny, mustard seed of faith.

I sat in my pew welling up with belief again. We continued to visit over the next weeks and then months. No matter what doubt or disbelief I felt Monday through Saturday, Sunday watered my seed. The "real presence of Jesus" in communion stirred so much hope in me.

Then one day I overheard my six year old daughter telling her friend that Jesus and God and the Holy Spirit were all one called the Trinity, and if you didn't love God you would go to hell.

I cringed.

What a horrible thing to believe, a horrible thing to teach my child! It sounded so painfully idiotic, and downright offensive, coming from the lips of a six year old. I realized then and there that I truly had been deceiving myself these past few months. I wanted to believe that my faith was returning so badly that I allowed myself to be swept up in the precious, sweet sentiment of it all. But when spoken of in the light of day, so plainly, so academically, I knew I didn't believe a word of it. I had to admit to myself that no matter what emotions Sunday stirred within me, Monday through Saturday were the days that mattered. And I flat out did not believe this.

In a last ditch effort, I turned to Pastor Mac. He exuded compassion and genuineness; I knew I could trust him. Before service the following Sunday, I caught his attention, and with stinging eyes, asked if I could speak to him sometime soon. I sat through the entire service fighting back tears.

As always, though, Monday came around, and I didn't want to talk to him anymore. I was supposed to call him, but I chose not to. The man is a good pastor and truly caring, so I wasn't surprised when he called me instead. I almost didn't want to answer the phone but took it as a sign from God. This was my last ditch effort after all. Maybe it was the effort that God was going to use to restore my faith. My little mustard seed. So I answered.

We talked for a while. I told him I couldn't hold on any longer, that I had one foot out the Christian door, and I felt before I called the whole thing off, I ought to speak to a pastor. He was very understanding and rational, and he prayed for me over the phone. While he prayed, I tried to join in with my heart, but it really felt all too late. Too late. We agreed to try to meet at some point to talk more in depth, but we never did. Not for his lack of trying; I just realized it was too late.

I was crushed. The burden of unbelief was heavier than I could bear. I told myself one last time the Christian answers – *You're trying to do this too much on your own. You are trying to get to heaven by works not faith.* But there was no hope for the alternative. No God had answered my pleas. No faith was buoying me above the water. Sinking, crushed, burdened, I had been thrust into the sea with a millstone around my neck. I kicked and struggled, grasped around for anything that could keep me afloat, gulped for air. But there was nothing to hold onto. As I exhaled my last breath and sunk slowly to the bottom of the sea, I realized even if there had been some driftwood bobbing in the waters nearby, I would not reach for it. I no longer wanted this. I no longer wanted any of this.

God, you took too long. I have collapsed under this unbearable burden. After all, I'm only made of flesh, and you left me to carry this yoke all on my own.

Part 3
After

Chapter 1
The Fourth Stage of Grief

She Killed a Dragon in Her Sleep
She killed a dragon in her sleep
for doing things that dragons do.
He made her beg for many nights
but never dried her tearful eyes,
his silent breath still blowing fire
on every secret thought she thought.
Her childish hands on clumsy sword
chopped his head right off his neck.
The smoking swirls had singed her curls
while conquering her greatest foe.
No longer would his smooth hot skin
Refuse her own a warming touch.
She sheathed the sword, black blood and all
And set it by his steaming breast,
Then she lay behind his back
And held him while she wept with rage.

I THOUGHT AT THIS POINT I'd arrived somewhere. If the loss of faith was a grieving process, which it was, I had been through denial, bargaining, and depression. I was now reaching acceptance, bypassing anger altogether. What did I have to be angry about anyway?

I thought long about my past. I wasn't angry that I'd been raised a Christian. My parents taught me about Jesus, because they believed in him wholeheartedly and wanted the best for me. Of course they would raise their offspring to place their treasures in heaven and aspire for eternal salvation. How could I be angry about that? I didn't regret anything that I'd been taught or gone through because of Christianity. Parts of my past hurt, but as far as I could tell, faith had gotten me through it. Of course, it also made me do things

I cringed over now, like the time I admitted to my favorite singer/songwriter Eleni Mandell, on that incredible night I actually got to hang out with her and her band, that yes, unfortunately, I believed she, as a Jew, would not be in heaven because she did not believe Jesus was the Messiah, or the time I said the same thing to my boss Wade at the bar I where I worked because he asked. But in general I was thankful for what Christianity had done for me. It took me to Scotland where I met my husband. It got me through bouts of depression and sorrow as an adolescent. All the journal entries and poems I used to write, all my sorrows splashed onto lined books with pretty covers, the ink smeared with my tears, had been interspersed with God's promises and prayers, and while there may have been some false piety in them, that faith in God had still gotten me through.

It kept me out of trouble. Christianity meant that "True Love Waits", and while I had some close calls, it meant I was a virgin on my wedding day. Without Christianity, I was certain I would have slept with all the many boys who I wanted to believe loved me, that I wanted to please, that I needed approval from. It meant that smoking pot and taking ecstasy were considered sins and had made me stop after only a year of experimentation. It kept me from more dangerous drugs, not for my safety's sake, but because of the frowning God who turned his face away from such transgression. It kept me from filing my taxes dishonestly and running my businesses unethically. It kept my reputation clean, and should I ever turn to a career in politics, I would have Christianity to thank for my shortage of closeted skeletons. What was there to be angry about?

Scott and I had lost touch with our old friends Jonathan and Sarah. We hadn't seen them in seven or eight years. With the advent of Facebook, we reconnected with them somewhat by the click of the Add Friend button but hadn't actually spoken to them. A rumor eventually reached us that Jonathan had left his post as pastor of his church and was back working in IT. Scott and I wondered what this meant, if there was any significance there. We later heard further rumors that they had left Christianity altogether. How coincidental.

Wanting to know the truth, I contacted Jonathan online. After pleasantries, I tentatively turned the conversation around to the rumors – were they true? They were. With relief, and a little excitement, I confided that I too was on the brink of leaving, and that Scott already had. I told him my story. It was liberating to announce the truth for the first time to an outsider. He asked if I felt any anger towards my past religious life. I said no. I had nothing to be angry about. Christianity had kept me out of a lot of trouble, I explained to him.

I could almost imagine him raising an eyebrow and cocking his head unconvinced from his own keyboard on the other side of the USA as he typed, "Hmm... Okay."

It wasn't until a few weeks later that a quiet rage simmering underneath surfaced. It only boiled over every now and again, and not too hotly, but it was simmering all the while. I first detected it when I went out for drinks with a Christian friend. She was telling us about some of the things she had done as a marriage counsellor and someone remarked what a good person she was. She cast her eyes down solemnly and said, "Not really, but thanks." She did not believe it. I knew she didn't believe it and wasn't just being modest; I knew it because that's how I always felt. She was a fellow spiritual masochist. Any good that we did, any right decisions that we made, any people we helped, none of it deserved any personal recognition, because at the end of the day, we were filth and anything good we did came from God, not us. We were sinful beings that God could not deign to look down upon without the covering of Jesus' blood. I could see this in her. I could also see her mentally recalling all the wrong she had ever done or was doing, all the poor choices, all the people she couldn't help or didn't try to help. All the things she needed to change about herself outweighed any perceived good she might have been recognized for.

I wanted to shout "But you ARE good!" I thought back on my own life, my own right decisions, the people I helped. All I ever tried to be, even with all the mistakes I made along the way, was good. And I really was good! It wasn't until that moment that I realized I'd been put down by my faith my whole life and made to believe I was inherently evil. The times when I dared to recognize that I had done something worthy or noble, I shot myself right back down for having too much pride. Pride proved that the state of my heart was still just as sinful and broken as ever.

All the ways I imagined Christianity had saved me, I was starting to realize, were actually not the case. There had always been an assumption that without God, I'd have been an evil, sinful, raping-and-killing maniac. But was that true? My parents taught me to respect myself, be confident in saying no when I didn't want to do something, to be honest and trustworthy, and to care about other people's feelings. What if actually, with all the exact same good guidance my parents had given me, minus the religion, I still would have turned out just as well?

While listening to NPR on his way to work, Scott was introduced to a band from Austin, Texas called Quiet Company, who were being interviewed on "All Things Considered" about their new album *We Are All Where We Belong*. He sent me a link to their website to download the audio, and it quickly became the soundtrack of my life. Every song put words to the unutterable emotions I was experiencing. One song in particular outlining the songwriter's own experience of losing his faith spoke volumes to me. At the end of the song, Taylor Muse sings:

> "Luckily I held out long enough to see
> Everybody really makes their own destiny
> It's a beautiful thing, it's just you and me, exactly where we belong...
> And there's nothing inherently wrong with us."

Those last words freed me. There's nothing inherently wrong with me! All my life, I'd lived with this underlying belief that I was broken, sinful, inherently evil, and unable to do any good without God. Little did I realize until then how deeply it had affected my entire sense of self. It was emancipating. It was also infuriating.

The bubbling volcano of anger would go on to erupt spontaneously over unexpected stimuli for several months. Driving down the road one night after my daughter's soccer practice, a bumper stick on the car in front of me read "I Will Never Leave You Nor Forsake You", and I screamed at the top of my lungs "*It's not true!*", slamming my fists against the steering wheel. A billboard on the freeway read "Where are you going? Heaven or Hell" and I wanted to jump out of my car and tear it down. I could never go back to that way of thinking. Even if I did come back around to having faith, I could never have faith in all of it, especially not hell. I found myself getting heated while reading an article written by a pastor about why people leave the church and the faith. Though I sympathized with his ignorance on the matter, I myself having been like him for decades, I was hotly annoyed by how simplistic and egotistical his proposals were. If anyone realized the sheer agony I'd been through for the past two and a half years, they wouldn't be able to take it so lightly or flippantly. They wouldn't be able to safely put me in a box and lock me away, saying I'd "never really believed in the first place" or I'd "never really understood". Being put in that box infuriated me. Unlike what they would prefer to believe, I wasn't a seed scattered on the path or sown amongst the thorns or cast into the rocky places.[16] Rather, I over-searched my heart, ripped apart all the layers in search of the truth. I believed in God and the Bible in spite of my conscious, intellectual doubts, and I never lied to myself about those doubts. I took my ability to still believe as a gift from God, for I knew God had chosen the foolish things to shame the wise.[17] Strip the gift of faith away though, and I was left with oozing open wounds that I still tore and slashed at, amongst my cries and tears, trying to find the meaning in the injury. Where's the heavenly purpose for that in the Bible? Somewhere in Job, where God made a terrible bet with Satan and ruined a man's life just to prove he could win?

I was now certain that few comfortable Western Christians had ever been to the excruciating lengths I'd been to keep my faith alive. I reflected on my entire life through a lens of anger. I contemplated all the years spent flagellating myself in the name of God to remind myself that I was nothing without him, and then how upon being thrust into my crisis of faith, God vanished into silence. How I then proceeded to claw away at myself to find some living cell within my incurable faith on which I could rebuild a self I didn't even want anymore, all so that I could still be pleasing to him. I was a battered wife, desperately trying to understand what I'd done wrong, on my knees, hands clasped, weeping pathetically for my lover to come back, trying uselessly to become who he wanted me to be, even long after he had abandoned me. I was beaten and bruised, half by my own spiritual masochism and half from the words written in his holy Word. I'd been left to die with no savior to rescue me.

I'd prematurely assumed I'd by-passed the anger stage, but there I was, boiling over, angry that God had abandoned me when I always believed he never would, never could. *If there is a God at all*, I thought, *I am his play thing, a useless toy he enjoys torturing for his own amusement like an unruly child.*

Chapter 2
The Snake and the Stone

I'M SHAMEFULLY ADDICTED TO SOCIAL media. I love looking up old friends and finding out what they have turned out like. Some have gotten married, some have successful careers, some are living life on the edge, and some are foreign missionaries. Often the ones I expected to have gone awry are the ones with the most ordinary, successful lives.

Some of their lives make me jealous. If they became deep sea divers and live in Jamaica, their lives seem so much more adventurous than mine. Some are living the dreams I always dreamed of, like playing in a rock band, or delivering babies as a midwife, or writing as a full-time profession. I mean, I love my life; I love the things I've done, and I'm proud of my accomplishments. I moved to Scotland where I lived for nine years married to a handsome Scotsman. I have three awesome children. I developed several home businesses. I free-lanced as a travel writer for an established tourism website. I like to imagine other people being impressed by me when they see my profile.

What made me most jealous during this time though were the people with fulfilling Christian lives. I don't mean the people who uploaded seascape images to Instagram with inspirational quotes about God scrawled across the top or who posted the "Bible Verse of the Day" on Facebook. I mean the people who were out in the world, doing awesome things, making a difference, all because they had a meaningful relationship with Christ.

It made me sad. It made me mad.

I wasn't sure at first what about it angered me so much. All I knew was that foreign feeling welling up within me that made me want to scream without knowing at whom or to what. Again, I wasn't angry with my parents for raising me in the faith. Having been a Christian for so long – thirty years – I completely appreciated and sympathized with the choice to raise one's children to believe in Jesus. I had been raising my children the same way. Evangelical Christians believe Christ is the only way to heaven, and without Christ, all others will suffer eternity in hell. It's a horrifying concept, and it's something Christian parents never want to imagine happening to their children.

My parents took me and my brothers to church every Sunday – no days off for fun – and demonstrated faith in their lifestyles. There was no other option, and even though we all got the opportunity to make our own decisions later on, the foundation was laid. After all, "raise a child in the way he should go, and he will not depart from it".[18] There was never any intent to coerce us, only the fervent desire to lead us onto the path of righteousness, which culminates in life everlasting. How could I be angry at them for wanting their children to live in harmony, die in peace, and spend eternity in heaven?

I wasn't angry with the church as a whole either. I had both bad and good experiences with church. I also recognized that churches could never be perfect. I did have some anger towards certain church practices though. Indeed I suffered a few incidents of "church abuse" or "spiritual abuse" at times, incidents where the church had used its power or influence to manipulate me.

I began reevaluating such incidents from my past. Particularly since rededicating my life at eighteen, but even much of my life before that, I'd wanted nothing more than to serve my God to the fullest and love Jesus with all my heart, soul, and mind. In college, my charismatic church believed in modern day use of the "gifts of the Holy Spirit" including Prophecy, Speaking in Tongues, and Healing. I was dubious at first about these things, but the testimonies of trusted friends who claimed to have seen miraculous healings and supernatural occurrences, such as deformed legs straightening before their very eyes or faces glowing with heavenly light as they shared the gospel, had opened me up to the idea. I believed my calling was ministry, either to addicts or to Muslims. It had all seemed to fit into a plausible grand master plan for my life: Pakistan, studying Arabic in college, and a church that had recently found its own calling in witnessing to Muslims, or Teen Challenge, Scotland, and my drug-addled friends. It all appeared well-orchestrated by God. We well knew from the missionaries we supported in Muslim countries and from the addicts who had been through rehab programs, that these were no easy callings. Bringing both Muslims and addicts to Christ required a lifetime of patience, very small results and a hefty dose of spiritual power.

One Sunday during my freshman year of college, I visited my aunt's charismatic church while home for a weekend. I sat in a congregation of two hundred or so while people stood at random speaking in tongues (which sounded to me like gibberish). In my heart, I tried to be open-minded though I was still very conflicted. I was raised in very conservative churches; my childhood churches never did anything like this. The preacher began prophesying over various people in the audience. This appeared to be the normal order of service. Tongues, Interpretation of Tongues, and Prophesy before the sermon. The preacher returned to the pulpit to begin his message; then he turned and looked me straight in the eyes, nine or ten rows back. He began climbing over the chairs to get to me, passionately crying, "You think all of this is false! You were brought up to believe these things aren't real, but I'm here to tell you that the Lord wants you to know it IS real and it IS from him!" He laid his hands on me and began praying in tongues. People all around me were crying, hands from all around were being laid on me. I myself was mesmerized and moved. How could he know? Did I show it on my face? I didn't think so, but either way, I believed his message was really from God, and I was touched that had God spoken to unimportant me. My aunt wiped away tears from her seat on the stage in the choir.

This particular event was not necessarily what I considered "spiritual abuse"; as far as I knew, there was no damage done. It was a positive experience and did not appear to be calculated. For me, the event only laid the foundation for further abuses, for that moment turned me into something of a hesitant charismatic believer. The official term is "non-cessationist" ("cessation" referring to the ceasing of these particular gifts after Jesus' ascension back into heaven after his resurrection). A couple of years later, when I traveled back to the United Kingdom to work with the addicts in Teen Challenge, I visited a charismatic Welsh church. After explaining my trip's purpose to an inquisitive woman next to me, I was surprised to be asked, "Are you filled with the Holy Ghost?" Well, yes, I told her. I was a Christian, had been for a long time.

No, she insisted. There was a difference between being a Christian and being filled with the Holy Ghost. She meant had I actually been filled with the Holy Ghost *as evidenced by speaking in tongues*. Awkwardly, even slightly guiltily, I replied I had not. She vehemently insisted that there was no way I could work with drug addicts (let alone Muslims) without the indwelling of power from the Holy Ghost. She laid hands on me and began shouting out to God, madly, half English, half gibberish. She wept huge, wet tears on my behalf, and applied so much pressure to my head that my neck ached. She cried out loudly for the Holy Ghost to enter me and give me the gift of tongues so I could fulfil his purpose on earth. I was terrified. I was also highly agitated and spinning with confusion. I felt her approach was violent and inappropriate yet the concept was perplexing. Why, actually, hadn't I been able to speak in tongues? So many other people I was close to could, why couldn't I? I left that service very upset, to put it mildly.

That night in bed I stared up at the ceiling unable to sleep. *Why, God, can't I speak in tongues? I want to have your power. I want all the good things you can give me. I want to my whole life to be yours. Please, give me this power. Please, give me the gift of tongues.* I slipped silently out of bed and laid prostrate, my face to the floor, in the dark guest bedroom of my host's flat. I pleaded with the Holy Spirit (the word "Ghost" seemed too creepy) to "intercede for [me] with wordless groans".[19] I felt very light headed and dizzy. I waited. I opened up my heart to anything the Lord had for me. The room was black and swirling. I could feel something gurgling within me, the tell-tale sign according to the testimony of others that tongues was soon to come upon me. I opened my mouth to allow the words to spill out as I'd been instructed and... Nothing. Nothing came. The room stopped spinning. The night was ordinary. I was just a girl lying face-down on the carpet like a lunatic. My heart broke. I just wasn't godly enough to be given such a precious gift.

Recalling that incident, I was incensed to think how religion had shoved my face in the dirty carpet and broke my spirit. I quickly came to realize after the incident that the woman had been entirely wrong in her treatment of me and that each person is granted a different spiritual gift. I reconciled later by returning to cessationism. I did not then blame God for that woman's conduct. However, I could not excuse her nor all the others who have treated people thus, for not everyone is able to bounce back. Too many people are beaten down continuously by this kind of behavior, and that made me angry.

I realized I was also angry at the way some churches and Christian organizations treated sinners. While they all confess to be made up of sinners themselves, their very doctrines and practices confirm there is no place in the church for the unsaintly. The Brethren actively practiced excommunication, and while on paper (Biblical paper anyway), I had agreed with the concept, I'd always hated the way it was administered in practice. It was one of the church doctrines that had me and Scott reaching for the exit door so many times. Alexander, for instance, had been a drug addict for many years but had finished the rehab program loosely affiliated with our church and was now a sober, professing, active Christian. One day, he confessed to his mentor at the rehab that he had started sleeping with his girlfriend. Old habits die hard. He wanted prayer. His mentor was obligated, by conscience and contract, to report this information to the rehab, since Alexander was still affiliated with the organization as a volunteer. Not only was Alexander immediately excommunicated from the church, he was also banned from the rehab's premises, and his mentor was banned from having any contact with the depraved sinner. The man had been a thieving, violent drug addict when they loved him, but all it took was sex to turn him into a degenerate. When the mentor refused to stop seeing Alexander in his own free, non-work, time, the mentor was fired from his job. No case was ever made against the organization for employment misconduct, since the mentor did not want to stir up trouble and destroy the "good" the organization was doing.

This type of abuse enraged me. It was beating the weak with a rod of self-righteousness to coerce perfect obedience.

The more I thought about it, there were actually so many things I was angry about. I became angry at how women were treated in my church. My whole life I'd accepted the lie that women were somehow inferior, unauthorized to preach because of our spiritual weakness borne of Eve. For years I'd worn a hat to symbolize my unworthiness to bear my head in communication with God, and even though I'd never personally believed head coverings were necessary, I went right along with it, silently teaching my own daughters to be silent where men tell you to be silent. I kept my mouth shut out of respect for men and doctrines that had no respect for me. I remembered a Sunday morning when a first time visitor attended our Remembrance service not donning a hat. During the men-only prayer time, she stood up and gave out a beautiful prayer. Scott and I had looked sidelong at each other under our bowed heads and gave each other satisfied and slightly rebellious grins. Inwardly, I wanted to stand up and cheer for this woman for praying out loud, unaware of our archaic church rules, because she was right. Then I recalled how upset I was to see the church leaders approach her at the end of the service and explain to her that she was not allowed to pray out loud because of the tiny little issue of her being a woman. Naturally she never came back. Despite my indignation, I still never said a word in protest, still kept my head covered and my lips sealed.

I was also angry on behalf of the people who were being financially abused by religion, not just by the corrupt television preachers who scam old people out of their pensions, who weekly convinced my own grandparents to send in their small social security checks promising healing for my grandmother via telephone prayer, but by all churches who shame their members and visitors into putting money into a basket to "further the kingdom". Christians are promised that by giving away a whole ten percent of our income ("it's not much!" the rich man insists), we will not only be perfectly provided for, but we will see God blessing us in countless ways, both financially and spiritually. We are told it is a privilege to go without.

I was burdened by this for years. When our first daughter was born, I quit my job so I could stay at home and raise her. Scott and I were committed to making this work, for this little girl was our world, and we wanted to be the ones to raise her. My husband, a young man just starting his career, made enough to pay our bills and little else. We stopped eating out, seeing movies, and going on shopping sprees. (We stopped buying expensive dishwasher tablets.) Some nights, we ate beans on toast for dinner because we couldn't afford more. When car troubles hit, or the baby needed bigger clothes, we panicked. There was nothing left.

And I couldn't afford to tithe.

Pastors preached sermons that convinced me our financial troubles were caused by our lack of faith to tithe. Yet I didn't dare bring up tithing with Scott; he was under enough pressure just to bring in enough for us to survive on, let alone to help fund the church's minibus or the preacher's salary. Instead, I suffocated under the strain of spending even less, reconsidering my stay-at-home-mum situation, and not giving to the Lord. I imagined myself as the widow with the mite; if I could just give a little bit, God would reward my obedience. But come Sunday, the five pound note in my pocket was equal to five cans of peas or two breasts of chicken, and as I looked into the eyes of my baby, I knew where that five pounds had to stay. Even as the guilt consumed me.

My parents took that weight of guilt off my shoulders. They reminded me that a tithe was giving up a portion of our "fortunes" to God's work. He then reminded me that I had given up not ten percent, but my entire salary – to raise our daughter. The tithing noose loosened, and I never put it back on again.

Financial abuse. Spiritual abuse. Female subjugation. As it turned out, I did still have anger towards aspects of church and religion.

But my greatest anger? My greatest anger was at God.

God promised me something. In the Bible, he promised that if I ask, it will be given. If I seek, I will find. If I knock, the door will be opened to me. The author asked, "What man, when his son asks for bread, will give him a rock? Or if he asks for a fish, will give him a snake?"[20] He is specifically referring to God's children, his chosen ones. The elect. Me. I asked. I sought. I knocked. Yet I never received, I never found, and Jesus never opened the door for me.

My heavenly Father gave me a stone.

He was supposed to be the Father in heaven who gives good gifts to his children, yet he gave me a stone! I was furious that God had abandoned me. I was furious that religion had made me desperate for something I couldn't have. I couldn't believe that what I lived my life for, this God I dedicated my life to, sacrificed for, had left me wallowing in desperation, alone and broken. I was now a lost sheep with no shepherd searching for me, cut off from a path I had been walking for over thirty years. I had nowhere to go. I was lost, wandering aimlessly in a life that was crushing in on me like the walls of Jericho. God lied to me. God abandoned me. God shut the door in my face and locked the deadbolt, instead of opening it when I knocked.

The lives of some old acquaintances found through social media made me feel a little wistful. But those of whom I was most jealous were the ones who still had their faith. The ones who still had an "intimate relationship with Jesus". The ones who still felt God's presence in their lives, who were still guided by his voice, who had not been abandoned by him. I envied them the most. If only I could have what they have!

But no. I didn't want it anymore. I'd seen through the haze, the lies, the myth; I'd seen the truth. There is no God. At least not the kind of God I always believed in. The God I believed in didn't abandon his children. He didn't hand them a stone when they were hungry for bread, or a snake when they asked for fish. I knew now he wasn't who I believed him to be, because there I was, standing with a stone in one hand and a snake in the other.

Chapter 3
No Fear In Love

The End Times
I know about the end times
because when I was young
I heard talk about brimstone and fire.
My dad in camouflage.
Mom looking at her watch.

I HAD ADMITTED I DIDN'T believe. I knew it was over. And yet I still just couldn't let it go.

I was so ready to close that chapter of my life, the same way I closed the chapter on being single and looking for love, or the chapters before children, or the chapters when my parents were married before their divorce, or the Scotland years. I could turn the page and start a fresh new chapter, blank and waiting for new words, and it would only marginally evoke a sigh.

I wanted to change my Facebook status to "Religion: None". I wanted to officially wave goodbye to our Lutheran church, with an apologetic hug to Pastor Mac who just wanted the best for us. I wanted to start answering my children's impossible questions about God the same way I answer their questions about Santa Claus: "You know it's just pretend, honey." I wanted to pack up my Christian friendships in a suitcase, at least the ones I knew wouldn't stick once they found out the truth, and leave them at the front door of the Goodwill. I wanted to hop a plane out of Jesusville and travel to a new world where all the other Religion: Nones hang out. I wanted to send a mass email out to all my loving, Christian family members declaring, "I am not a Christian anymore. Please respect my decision and do not ask me about it ever again." I wanted to take the two crosses off my wall, and the plaque that read "As for me and my house, we will serve the Lord".[21] I wanted to take the Bible that remained perpetually in the back seat pocket of the driver's side of my car, and all my Christian self-help and theology books, and donate them to a used book store. I wanted to escape that false persona of me as a struggling saint and step into the blinding light, naked, blinking, with pupils constricted, as me, as just me, the failed pietist, the *homo sapien*.

But for some reason, I couldn't. The flesh is willing, but the spirit is weak. What was holding me back from walking away? I was like a bull held back by a gate, huffing and snorting and stomping, ready to charge ahead and tear down whatever got in my way. I wanted to run, full-speed ahead, everything be damned, but something held me back.

I questioned what held me back every day for weeks. The spiritual masochist wouldn't leave it alone; it just picked at the scab until it bled a little more. It had no time to wait for healing. My knee-jerk reaction was always to assume it was God. Maybe, just maybe, God was the one still holding me back. It made sense, and I liked that idea. It fit in with all my theology, that I was not the last petal of the tulip falling, that I was still persevering and would until the very last, even if ever so slightly. It also meant I had not been abandoned after all. It meant all this had not been in vain but would eventually take me to a new place, a real place, one where God and Jesus and the Holy Spirit still reside. I liked that idea. It felt spiritual and comforting and safe. In moments where I really almost believed that, I felt something akin to peace. I gripped my fingers around those moments until my knuckles turned white.

When my fingers relaxed, however, everything came rushing back to me:

Jesus said if I knocked, the door would be opened.

Jesus said he'd return before the end of that generation.

I had no evidence for God except a book compiled by countless different people's writings over many centuries – that claims wild and fantastic things that no one would believe if written anywhere else – and was finally compiled in the canon by a council of men several hundred years after Jesus' death, who threw out the parts that didn't fit until they had a mostly concise story.

That book, thus declared the inspired word of God, is misogynistic and patriarchal.

God created a hell for people who didn't believe, who didn't know they were supposed to believe, and who weren't capable of believing. He also sends people there who have asked for faith but whose requests have been denied. By him. (Like me.)

The list went on, but by the time all these things had hit me again, I would have already swallowed another painkiller to ease the headache.

Even if God was holding on to me, it didn't change the fact that I could no longer take on all these burdens of belief. I could not assimilate them into my life and my understanding of what goodness is. I could not shift enough paradigms to make it all work. If God did give me back the gift of faith now, would I even accept it? The oxygen I so desperately longed for had turned to poisonous gas. I didn't want it anymore.

So what then, what was holding me back?

As a child I had prayed many times to ask Jesus into my heart. One of those times was when my grandparents took me to their Assembly of God church to see a play which portrayed the stories of various people in their last moments of life and their subsequent first moments of eternity. Will they walk through the gates of heaven or will they succumb to the flames of hell?

The good people, and perhaps one bad person who at the end of his life begged for salvation, all met a meek, white-robed, shaggy- haired Jesus who graciously and lovingly drew them to the shining bright light on Stage Left where they would spend eternity in peace, comfort and eternal bliss. The bad people, however, and maybe one person who "thought" he was good, were dragged kicking and screaming to where red satin streamers flapped onto the stage by the fan of the flickering red lights of hell, Stage Right. The moral of the story: You never know when your last moment will be (car crash, falling to your death in a freak accident, gunshot, or if you're simply lucky, old age), so get prepared now. Ask Jesus into your heart now (there will be an altar call at the end of this production to assist you as you make your lifelong commitment now) or risk dying on the way home and being dragged to your eternal doom by the scariest red Spandex-wearing, black goatee-sporting Satan you could ever imagine.

At the end of that production, when the pastor asked the non-believers in the crowd to raise their hands to be saved – and requested that the rest of the audience bow their heads so they wouldn't see whose hands were raised – I nervously lifted my hand. I had already asked Jesus into my heart a couple of times before, but now I had to be sure, doubly sure, triply sure that I was saved, just in case. I did not want to be dragged Stage Right. I was terrified of being dragged Stage Right, for all of forever, never to be released. My Mamaw next to me gently tugged my arm back down. I was so confused. Was she ashamed that I wasn't already saved? I was afraid of disappointing her so I put my hand down and stayed in my seat. I remembered that I could just as easily get saved from my seat as from the altar, so there in my chair, I begged God to please save me from going to hell, but I was still afraid that by not actually getting out of my seat and going forward, that my pride had kept me from actually being heard by God.

I was eight years old.

Hell.

What if one day I discovered all of this actually is true, God is real, and the Bible is his precious Word? What if I realize all of that, but all too late for my children? By then, my pagan, sin-loving children will have no sense of God, no interest, and will be on their way straight to hell, all because I didn't raise them right. I myself could be fixed, if need be, but the hell-bound souls of my own flesh and blood would be on my hands for all eternity. What about all the rest of the damage my apostatizing would do? All the people whose faiths I might shake, all the hurt and pain I would cause my loved ones, all because I couldn't look God square in the eye – or rather because I tried to look God square in the eye – and couldn't face my own sin and blame as a result.

What if I'm wrong, and I go to hell?

That thought halted me dead in my tracks. It always had. It was the same terror I'd lived with all through childhood. Here once again the panic rose up around me. Blanched the skin on my face. Stopped time. The terror of it. The sheer horror of living with Satan gloating and laughing in my immortal face, the orange flames of desolation and regret licking my body, my groaning and wailing, surrounded by the discordant orchestra of groaning and wailing from fellow doubters and detractors, misery, agony, separated from all joy and good and God for eternity with no chance to make amends, forever and ever and ever and ever... and ever...

This. This is what stopped me. This was my clanking metal gate curtailing the bull's escape to freedom. I was terrified of hell. I was terrified of the risk that not-believing put me at. If I denounced God, this eternal damnation was my fate, my future. I could stop believing in the entire Bible with little discomfort, but fear, terrifying fear of hell, left me stone cold and paralyzed. I was stuck between that notorious rock and hard place, unable to go back but afraid to go forward. One way lead to a life of perpetual self-delusion, the other to everlasting fire and brimstone. The next step was crucial. It might be Game Over if I turn Judas, hell fire awaiting as I step off the precipice. Or I might just discover that indeed it all was only a game, and I didn't have to play it anymore. Either way, the next step seemed impossible to take.

I went back to see a production of that same play I'd seen as a child. I wanted to know if it was really as frightening as I remembered. It was. Everything was exactly as I remembered it, except Satan wasn't wearing red Spandex as he did in my mind's eye, but instead a black cloak, a menacing mask with evil facial features and had reverb in his loud, booming voice. Hell was still Stage Right, with smoke and satin flames and flickering red lights. He still dragged both bad and good (though all of course always *pre-warned*) people into his lair, begging and screaming their bloodcurdling pleas for forgiveness all too late. Even as a thirty-something year old, I watched in horror, as my chest tightened with memories of that childhood terror, the childhood dreams of demons dragging me to hell, the fear I was never really saved and would one day die to hear my supposed Savior shout, "Depart from me, I never knew you!" Unchecked, I myself would've been swayed by the naked fear it instilled in me; that primal fear of hell may never go away.

It was a sad realization. The trauma we go through as children will always be with us. It will always be there, hidden in somewhere in our psyches, long after rationalization and logic take over our conscious thoughts.

There were several children in the audience, some who looked too young to even be in school. To their credit, the production staff did warn at the start that the program was not suitable for children under ten and encouraged parents to send their kids to a children's program located elsewhere in the building. Many kids went to that, but many stayed. I wondered how many parents who kept their kids with them had actually seen the play themselves previously. I wondered if they had, if they would still insist on keeping their children in to watch teen suicides, domestic violence, murders, car and plane crashes, school shootings, and of course the Devil Himself unfold right before their baby eyes.

My heart ached when I saw a tiny little girl, no older than six, lift her own skinny arm at the altar call at the end, seeing myself in her tiny blond bob, seeing her future before her. Fear will be with her as she grows into a woman.

After the final scene, where a screaming unsaved mother is dragged away from her screaming, begging Christian teenage daughter by the billowy, echoey hooded Satan and his demons at the gates of heaven, and the girl is hugged by Jesus then sent on her own to enter the pearly gates looking forlorn but okay, the production director came on stage and began the obligatory altar call. At first, he asked that all would bow their heads and close their eyes, just as the director did twenty-five years ago. He asked that anyone who wanted to invite Jesus into their lives slip a hand in the air. He then asked them to stand, and anyone else who was too afraid to lift their hands the first time to also stand. Then he requested that all the backslidden Christians stand. Even with my head bowed, I could sense all the bodies around me standing. He then invited them to come forward to the altar at the front. Bodies filed past me, many crying, many looking guilt-ridden, a few looking relieved. As the director kept insisting there were more backsliders who hadn't yet come forward, and more "backsliders" filed past me to the front, I felt the same familiar rage build inside of me. *These are good people! You are all good people!* I wanted to scream. I was angry at the guilt heaped upon guilt being laid on thick on all the spiritual masochists in the room – and all the normal people too – who were all searching their hearts and determining that he – no, God – was speaking to them. I waited. I wanted to stay to the end if I could.

Then he said, "Christians, I want you to turn to the person next to you, even if you don't know them. Maybe put your arm around them. I want you to ask them, 'Do you know Jesus Christ as your personal Lord and Savior?' "

I couldn't take any more.

Before the sweet looking teenager next to me whose friend had just gone forward could turn to me, I turned to the aisle and marched not forward to the altar but backwards to the back of the room and out the back door. Eyes followed me, but I did not care. I had no intention of making a scene, but I'd seen and heard enough. Frustrated, I knew that many people interpreted that as me hardening my heart to the Spirit, but it was far from being that. It was like having to leave a scene of abuse that you have no way of stopping. Like having to walk away from something that is so wrong and out of your control that you cannot bear witnessing it any longer. Like turning your head away from a car crash on the freeway instead of rubbernecking. I had seen enough of my past and these strangers' futures to watch any longer. The anger bubbling up inside me was too explosive. I was afraid of what I would've said to that sweet teen next to me. Afraid of what would have come out of my mouth.

Luckily no one followed me outside, though I was terrified someone might.

Reflecting later that night, one more sad realization struck me. Fear is the overarching theme of this play. The scenes of people going to hell dominate not only my recollections of that night, but my memories of the play from twenty-odd years ago. I remembered so distinctly the damned being dragged to hell Stage Right. But how is it that I did not remember that the saved walked up a huge flight of stairs center stage to enter heaven through a shiny curtain at the top where they were greeted by Jesus? I had only concluded that the Christians went to heaven Stage Left because actually, I couldn't remember at all what happened to the saved. That was never the point of the play. How did I recall every detail of hell in the wings more than twenty years later but forgot that the entire stage was decorated in gold and silver, with sparkling steps running up the center, surrounded by angels who stood on stage *the entire time*, with a humble Jesus waiting at top, arms outstretched?

Jesus is not the point of this play, that's why.

Jesus never speaks a word. Not one word throughout the whole production. He never makes a single active motion aside from hugs to the people who climb the steps towards him. In only one scene does he seem to intervene in a situation at all, the one in which a troubled teen commits (accidental) suicide. Both Jesus and Satan approach her silently, then Satan flees when she calls out to Christ. Even then, Jesus only stands there smiling gently. He does not actually do anything for her until she is in heaven and he silently wipes his hand across her arm, removing the scars from years of cutting, before sending her through the curtain.

Conversely, Satan has lots to say. In his booming, echoing voice, he taunts the sinners, laughs at the arrogant fools who thought being a good person was good enough, and then addresses the audience with one-liners about how he loves to watch anger *CONSUME* people's hearts and how pornography is his *SPECIALTY*. Then he flaps back to hell with guffaws that echo through the room after blackout.

Jesus is entirely forgettable. I do not recall anything that Jesus did over twenty years ago on that stage. But Satan was everything I remembered, minus the Spandex.

"*There is no fear in love. But perfect love drives out fear, because fear has to do with punishment. The one who fears is not made perfect in love.*"(1 Jn 4:18)[22]

Chapter 4
Pascal's Wager Part 2: Esau I Have Hated

My fear of hell was diminishing. It had mostly disappeared, except that every now and then, fear still momentarily struck my heart. *I am literally playing with fire*, I'd think. I'd get a sense that I better repent quickly just in case it all turned out to be true after all.

What I will lose if I wager wrongly! There is an eternity of suffering waiting for me should I wager against God and be wrong. What do I lose by following God and there is no God? Very little. What do I lose by not following God should there be a God? Everything. On these little occasions, I panicked about how I had played my cards, as the fear of hell crept back up on me.

Pascal's Wager almost makes some sense, except the wager overlooks two important issues. First, it assumes that the only God worth wagering on is the Christian God, ignoring the possibility that a different religion might be the right one. Still, that issue aside, the second thing it overlooks is that without faith it is impossible to please God.[23] Yet faith is a gift from God, it is not of ourselves.[24] Therefore, I cannot please God without faith if he does not *choose to give it to me*. I could wager that God was real and keep following him as I had been doing for the past three years, but I would not be saved, for anyone who comes to him must believe that he exists.[25] Pascal's Wager is useless without faith.

Sadly, it was fear, not love, that sporadically warned me to reconsider God. God's love had been gone from my life for a long time. Abandonment and silence echoed in the cavern where love once dwelled. But fear could still make me draw in a sharp breath, as it sliced through my heart like a paper cut. When I paid this fear some attention, it gathered like a thundercloud inside my head and struck my conscience with forks of lightning. I asked myself, *Do you really want to bet your life on this and end up languishing in excruciating damnation for your sinful pride, your worldly "wisdom", your pitiful human understanding, for all eternity?*

Fear is a powerful tool. Yet if God's plan for restoring my faith was fear mongering, I was even less inclined to believe he was the God of Love I once knew – or thought – him to be. If it were the *love* of God striking my heart, drawing me to him, there would be something in it worth carefully considering. However, the fact that only the fear remained seemed psychologically obvious. It was neither God himself, nor his Holy Spirit, calling me back, but thirty years of religious manipulation. Hell is the scariest and most effective tool for keeping the righteous in check. Heaven's promise pales in comparison.

The revoked love of God in my life and the dubious possibility of heaven were not enough to draw me back to faith. The fear of hell and the almost certainty of God's wrath, however, left me quaking. With the cards of my still unfinished life lying on the table, I could still change how I placed my bets. Yet if the God of the Bible is the one true God, my bets don't matter in the slightest. God chooses whom he loves and whom he hates. He chose Jacob but hated Esau.[26] The cards on the table were never mine to choose from.

And we call this *agape*.

Chapter 5
An Icy Winter

THAT WINTER WAS PARTICULARLY ICY. I consider myself a fairly good bad-weather driver, so despite the sheet of ice and slush covering the roads one morning in February, I got in my car and slowly, cautiously headed into town to get some errands taken care of. The back roads were horrendous - nothing but refrozen ice. No cars passed. I assumed the main roads would be better, but as I approached the stop sign that joined up to the main road, with railroad tracks behind me, and a pond on either side of me, my car skidded. I tapped the brakes as one should, I correctly steered into the skid, but the ice was more than I could handle, and I couldn't control the car. At that very moment, two cars appeared out of nowhere, one on the main road at the perfect distance of upcoming intersection with my car and one behind me, also unable to stop and unable to swerve. My heart beat fast. I pulled out in front of the approaching car, while the car behind me skidded to the left of me. I spun sideways and finally stopped, my car facing the pond, inches away from the drop off, the oncoming car just able to slide past me. None of us collided. All three of us looked frightened.

I pulled into the nearest parking lot and slowly turned around. I was going home. Back on the road, I instinctively muttered, "Lord, keep me safe."

Then it hit me. Almost too joltingly it hit me for one driving on such treacherous roads. Prayer was meaningless. There was no one helping me. As quickly as that panic took hold of me, a reassurance filled its place. I was alone now, but then again, apparently I'd always been alone. And I'd always been able to drive safely. It was never God who'd been protecting me on icy roads; it was my own ability to drive defensively.

I felt confident from that point on that I'd make it home without an accident. All those years I believed my protection came from the Lord, it had been merely coincidence or my own capability. Praying did not keep me safe.

The same winter, a high school friend's dad died. The death was sudden and unexpected. Jenny flew in from out of state for the funeral. Her Facebook page was filled with heartfelt, well-meaning promises of prayers.

Death makes everyone uncomfortable. Praying – or at least promising to pray – is the standard response to news of a death. Even non-religious people will find the words coming out of their mouths. It is what we automatically say and what we expect to hear. I too have prayed for and promised to pray for friends who have experienced loss. It was all I knew to do. I would feel so helpless watching a friend grieve. Because we are powerless to do anything, we pray. We may not be able to take away their pain, but God could, so we believe our prayers to God will...

Will what?

Jenny's father's death caused me to think on this. What exactly did our prayers aim to do? Convince God to comfort our grieving loved ones? Wouldn't it be safe to assume that of course he was going to do that already?

Praying for a grieving friend is ultimately a self-centered act, I realized. If God's comfort to those in need is dependent upon my prayers, then God must be very lazy, and possibly quite cold-hearted. Since of course no one who believes in God believes he is too lazy or cold-hearted to comfort without our cajoling, the act of prayer is really just a way of pacifying our own feelings of helplessness.

I remember being taught that prayers are sometimes more about changing our own hearts and wills to become more aligned with the Father's than about changing God's mind or convincing him to act. Depending on one's theology (and this was my Calvinistic one), God's plan cannot be changed. Therefore prayer is less about getting what I want and more about letting God change my heart.

In bereavement, praying always made me feel better. Praying helped me sort out my feelings and fears about death, it helped me cope with what I realized was inevitable for me some day. It also made me feel like I'd done something significant to help ease someone else's pain.

Yet it did nothing for the sufferer.

If God exists as the God of the Christian faith, he will comfort his children in their sadness. He will be quick to respond to their needs, he will come speedily to their aid. With or without my prayers.

My prayers, therefore, accomplish only one goal: to make me feel better. How selfish.

I did not pray for my friend. I felt guilty about it. I felt by not praying, I was not loving her enough. I felt cold for not praying for her. But what would be the point? I was pretty sure there was not actually a God to pray to, and if by chance there actually was, my prayers would no more make him get up and go put his arm around her than if I didn't pray. Prayers of the faithless are not heard anyway.[27]

Prayer would have been the easy way out. It would have let me avoid any real confrontation of loss. I could pray far away in the comfort my own home while never looking Jenny in the eye. I'd be absolved from having to think of what to say or what to do; I'd never have to actually face anything. Meanwhile, the bereaved family would grieve alone, with an emptiness and agony they cannot imagine ever fading.

I am not comfortable with death. I don't know what to say. I don't know what to do. But perhaps learning not to pray helped me learn how to be a better friend. I considered the ways I could help. I could make her some food. I could send flowers or donate to a hospice on their behalf. I could drop off a bottle of vodka. I could write her a card or a letter. I could bring her a salad and sit with her while she talks or doesn't talk, cries or doesn't cry. I could actually do something that doesn't comfort me but might comfort her. My act of love might be small, but it would be action. It would be confrontation of my fears and her sorrow, rather than passive words that release me from further concern as soon as they are uttered.

I did not pray for Jenny. Instead, I bought a bag of groceries, knocked on her mother's door where she was staying, which was answered by her sister who didn't have a clue who I was, and awkwardly handed over the bag with the inept words, "Just so you don't need to go to the store."

I attended the visitation to support Jenny and be there for her in case she needed a friend to talk to. I and two others from our old high school gang offered her our condolences and sat two pews back, there for her if she needed us. I stared at the closed coffin with the American flag blanketed overtop. He'd been a sergeant in the US Air Force. He left behind five children. He had struggled in life.

I sat in silence shifting my attention from the coffin to the photo slideshow. A younger dad surrounded by small children. An aging father giving his daughter away to be married. A life taken too soon.

A man I barely knew. A near breaking atmosphere in the room, as if the air were made of eggshell. The disconcerting echo of his younger children giggling loudly, as if the reality had not hit them yet. The funeral home's predictably peach walls and burgundy carpets and pews, as if all funeral homes found the '70s to have the most consolatory decor.

A selfish relief filling me. For the first time, a funeral did not perplex me. I felt ashamed for thinking of myself during this time, but as I looked at that coffin, I realized something obvious but significant.

He was gone.

Not just from this life but from all life.

There was no afterlife to worry myself with. Yes, I said myself.

I've been to many funerals. Most were to remember fellow Christians who'd passed, but a few were for non-Christians, or not-quite-certain ones like Jacqui. At each funeral, what perplexed me most was my heartfelt worry over their eternal souls. Even the Christian deaths had me rubbing my knuckles in concern. Were they really saved? Are they definitely with Jesus now? Or is there a chance they were never really what we thought them to be and are now suffering the intolerable agony of hell fire and eternal separation from God?

It was worse at non-Christian funerals. The careful wording of the preacher, the tension and devastation we Christians felt, so engulfing was the reality of where this unbeliever now spent eternity, so unendurable that we preferred to believe they might have repented at the last possible second and had been spared. Those lost instantly in car accidents or heart attacks gave us less room for hope. Instead, the weight of their damnation clung to our consciences, so heavy, so final, that we shut our minds down, and our hearts, and rested discomfited in numbness.

At this funeral, I did not wonder if the man in the coffin, the aging father, the veteran, the man with worries, struggles, joys and accomplishments, was greeting Jesus in heaven or crying out in hell. I did not know what his faith was, or if he had a faith, but it did not matter. What mattered – and what aggrieved those around him – was that he was gone. His seat at the dinner table would be empty. His phone would ring and ring if dialed. His grandchildren would never know him. His passing was the sorrow, his departure from this life was the cause of pain, his family and friends left behind were the ones who needed my compassion and concern, not his soul. I was so used to worrying about the soul of the deceased at every other funeral I'd been to that I had no room left to truly consider how I might show compassion to the bereaved in their very present moment of loss.

Chapter 6
The Break-Up Song

THE LAST CHURCH SERVICE we ever attended was a few weeks before Easter. Our church attendance had already begun to wane, but now I felt no compulsion to go at all. I had accepted that I didn't believe in God or Jesus Christ anymore. However, my in-laws had flown in from Scotland to stay with us for six weeks. I have enormous respect and love for my in-laws, who were my substitute parents for nine years. I knew they'd want to see us happily settled in a church. So Scott and I kept going for their sake.

In my pretty Sunday dress and heels, I sat in the pew between my husband and my mother-in-law for the first time in weeks. It wasn't so bad. I liked being there, really. There was always a peaceful atmosphere in that little Lutheran church, and Pastor Mac was happy to see us again after months of absence.

The music started. One thing we always loved about church was the music. The song choice was lovely that day. We started with "Joyful, Joyful We Adore Thee". This was one of my favorite hymns; we sang it at our wedding. Scott and I sang with gusto, because we love to sing, and hymns are fantastic to sing along to.

Then came the liturgy. I tried to read along, but the words had become meaningless to me – worse than meaningless. They were phony. I felt extremely uncomfortable reciting creeds I didn't hold to and promises from Scripture I didn't believe in. Yet I didn't want my in-laws to guess what was inside my heart. I mumbled the words, as if mumbling made them less spoken.

We prayed. The prayers seemed to float to the ceiling, deflate, and fall lifelessly to the carpeted center aisle. They did not reach heaven. It occurred to me that should be sad in a way, but I wasn't sad at all. This charade meant nothing. We stood again to sing the next song, "In Christ Alone" by Stuart Townsend.

This was my favorite church song of all time. The tune is moving, the words are powerful. I started to sing along with the congregation, pleased to use my voice to sing such a beautiful tune.

But only a stanza in, I choked up. I had to stop singing for my voice was no longer stable. If I dared go on, the tightness in my throat, the wobble in my notes, the redness in my eyes would be noticeable. I read along silently while the singing continued around me, and I wondered what had upset me.

Was God trying to speak to me through this song? Was I holding back the emotion out of stubbornness? I contemplated this possibility seriously.

I supposed it could be true, though I doubted it. Then I considered a different possibility.

For years after my breakup with Dylan my junior year of college, even after being married to Scott, a certain Flaming Lips song never failed to bring tears to my eyes. I was no longer in love with Dylan, and I did not miss him. I did not wish we had gone ahead and gotten married. Yet the song stirred in me memories of a deep pain that I was sorry I ever had to feel. The song did not mean that I wanted Dylan back, but simply evoked those feelings of heartbreak that I endured during a painful time in my life.

This song too was a love song. It held a special place in my heart. Many spiritual blossoms grew out of singing this song. It hurt to sing it, because it represented a break-up.

I struggled to maintain my composure. It was a beautiful song. It contained beautiful sentiments. At best, I concluded, there was something beautiful and romantic about religion, but at the end of the day, it's all just beautiful fantasy. And I didn't want to hold onto fantasy, not anymore, no matter how beautiful it was.

Chapter 7
Seeing the Light

It was almost Easter. Driving into town to do some shopping, I struggled with the question of whether or not we should take the family to the Easter service at church as was tradition. It was the dawn of spring and after several weeks of snow and ice, the sun was shining and the birds were chirping.

I have an emotional connection with light. All my most memorable religious moments involved a bright light – as cliché as that is. Perhaps it's cliché because we all have that connection to light. Perhaps that's why light is so prominently featured in religious stories, why we "see the light" or when we die we "follow the light". My moment in Pakistan, asking for a sign, with the clouds parting and the sunbeams shining down on me. My rededication experience at The Grove where I felt God had doused me in light "better than drugs". In between those "big" light memories are many "small" light moments, where light is a main character in the story of my memory, such as opening my clinched eyes after hours of labor with my second daughter, to be surprised by the light and the presence of my child, or how every time I hear that one Imogen Heap song I remember how sunny and bright that day was when I first heard it driving down the motorway from Glasgow to Greenock.

Jonathan had once described coming out of Christianity like crawling out of a cave. When he said that, I felt it was more like being left in a desert or jumping out of a plane without a parachute. But now, as I drove down the highway, I suddenly felt like my eyes had been opened, like I was emerging from my cave and driving into the light. The sky was blue, the sun was bright, and I had another "light" experience. This time, however, it couldn't really be accurately called religious, because it was the undoing of religion that impressed its light on me.

I suddenly felt free. Freedom is a Christian's favorite emotion; we always talk about freedom in Christ, the truth shall set you free. I always felt free in that way. But this was different. I was suddenly convinced, utterly convinced, that God is made up, the Bible is an ancient text that made sense to ancient civilizations but is simply no truer than the Bagavagida or Gilgamesh. I realized, to my immense relief, that God never abandoned me at all – he simply *never existed*.

This truth set me free. Really free. I drove into this light, this pure, unreligious, scientific light of the earth's sun as we rotated around it in our orbit, and I basked in it. I did not know how long this clarity would last. Would I moments later return to uncertainty? Would I worry once more about hell and my salvation tomorrow? The light shining down on me, around me, through me, gave me hope. Strange, incomprehensible hope, for hope to me had always been found in the resurrected Christ, not the absence of God. Ironically, the experience was precisely the kind I'd been asking for from God for so long – a new God-moment to top all the other religious, life-changing God-moments in my life, except it was the concretely un-God-momentness of this that finally gave me peace after nearly three full years of anxiety and torment.

I still have half my life to live, and I don't need to spend it worrying about hell. I stepped out of my cave, blinking in the light. A huge smile spread across my face. I was free. I was *in the light*. I was at perfect peace.

I hadn't known peace like that in a very, very long time.

Afterword
Coming Out of the Closet

I'VE HEARD OF AILING PEOPLE making religious pilgrimages in hopes of finding physical and spiritual healing, like Muslims to Mecca or Catholics to Rome. In many ways, it is the sojourn which brings spiritual wellness to the sick. It is through the journey that we learn the greatest lessons in truth.

This book was my spiritual pilgrimage towards healing. As I crawled through the overgrown recondite forest of doubt, my knees burning and bleeding, my palms tearing at the twisted thorns and rocky soil, a quiet, unnoticed healing slowly took place. The written journey, the act of working through my fears and doubts, exploring my past and present with words on paper, was a balm to my broken flesh and bruised soul. It dragged me out of valleys and ditches threatening to sprain my ankles or break my bones, leaving me face down in the dirt of grief, and pulled me back up onto my feet. I started writing this book months before that drive down the highway, and perhaps it was the journey of writing that finally brought me to that clearing.

Still, months of internal processing passed after that drive. I had realized there was no god. I realized it down to the very marrow of my bones. All fear of hell and punishment had finally vanished. Now that fear was replaced with a new fear: how I'd be treated by my family and society. Here I was writing a book about my loss of faith, but I had yet to tell anyone in person that I now called myself an atheist.

When one leaves the Christian faith, it is something to be hidden. It is scandalous. In some places it might even be dangerous. In a Christian society, leaving the faith is most definitely not something to shout from the rooftops. While Christians would praise a Muslim for bravely coming out as Christian to his or her family (thereby likely being disowned, if not downright in danger of death), they cannot conceive of the reverse – a Christian coming out as Muslim, or perhaps a Mormon, and especially not an atheist. Announcing a conversion to Christianity is lauded but leaving the faith should be kept quiet.

More than anything I wanted to announce to the world that I was atheist.

I wanted to finally get it out in the open, so I wouldn't have to hide who I really was anymore. I didn't have any ulterior motive; I wasn't out to change anyone. I just wanted to be free. I wanted to be known.

But I was afraid.

I was afraid of losing my friends, my family, and my job.

I was afraid of hurting and humiliating my family. I was afraid of putting my children at risk of bullying.

The reality of it is, if you are not Christian - at least here in the Bible Belt - you are at risk. And to leave the faith is the worst thing a person can do. It makes Christianity look bad. It gives non-Christians more ammunition. It lends credence to the possibility that Christianity may not be the only answer. When I first published our letter of resignation from the Brethren Church on my blog, I was reproached for "giving Christianity a bad name". Many people felt what I had done was only furthering non-Christians dislike for Christianity. While I saw their point, I also saw the other side of it. Hiding the faults of churches furthers the non-Christian dislike for Christianity too, perhaps more so. We all know the bad press the Roman Catholic Church has gotten for brushing their perversions under a rug.

When I rededicated my life in college, I told everyone. I didn't want to hide it from anyone. Even in situations that felt awkward, where I felt I might lose a friend or make myself look foolish, I still made my faith known. I did not want to deny Jesus here on earth. I may have lost a couple of friends, though if I did, I never knew about it, because there was never any real backlash. I was accepted into a church and a society that congratulates such a decision, and everything was just grand. Some people thought I was a little nuts, but it didn't get much worse than that.

Unfortunately, I knew for a fact that if now I shared even a fraction of that kind of openness about my non-faith, there would be backlash. I knew I would hurt and humiliate my family. I knew I'd be unfriended on Facebook (by some friends and possibly even some family members). I suspected many of my other fears would become reality. There is such a stigma to being atheist. The word itself implies hedonism, arrogance, hatred, intolerance, and lawlessness. None of these words described me, but as soon as I were to give myself the atheist label, I would have given myself the rest of the labels too.

Some people knew I was no longer actively attending church, my mom specifically. The assumption was I had "fallen away" or "backslidden". A few other people knew I was "not religious" - mostly new people I'd met since moving back to Arkansas. Yet I feared that if I came out and used the A-word, they'd be really shocked, repulsed even.

I played around with semantics. I could publicly call myself "agnostic", but that implied a malleability that simply was not present. It sounded like I just didn't know but could be persuaded. It was a safer option, but with the connotations of this word, it wouldn't be true. I didn't need to give myself a label at all, but I felt I needed one. I'd been one label my whole life – Christian – and I wanted to rip that label off of me like those irritating, scratchy tags on t-shirts.

Scott and I were atheists, and at some point we'd have to face the music. Especially if I ever planned on this book seeing the light of day.

Speaking to my dad about my non-belief seemed to happen pretty easily. My dad is an intelligent man and a devout believer. One night, while sitting around the kitchen table, just the two of us, while the kids played with their step-grandma, we started talking about religion. It felt like the perfect opportunity to come clean. I began telling him about my loss of faith over the years. It seemed a totally rational discussion. He asked if I was still at least theist at all. I knew the answer was no, but I copped out and said I didn't know. I guess I was still afraid to admit my atheism completely. I left his house that night feeling a little lighter. He had taken the news well. Maybe this wouldn't be so bad after all.

However, later on, when I became openly *atheist* (online), he started spending a lot of (well-meaning) time trying to argue and debate with me, hoping to win me over with apologetics. The constant friction sometimes hurts, and though we are still trying to work through how to relate to each other with such a wide gap between us belief-wise, our relationship has not been ruined.

Talking to my mom was a lot harder. My mom is my best friend, and she is a devout believer too, but unlike my dad, her faith is very emotionally charged. The thought of broaching the subject with her made me want to run a mile. Yet the subject came up one day without me even realizing I'd provoked it.

On Facebook, I had asked openly what kind of information parents give their teens regarding birth control and sex. Naturally, with so many Christian friends, the subject went straight to no sex before marriage. I mentioned that abstinence was a great thing, and yes the Bible requires it, but it wasn't very realistic. I wondered how they dealt with the reality that most teens will not wait until marriage. This must have revealed more than I realized about my opinion of the Bible, for my mother asked me in a text message, "Do you no longer believe in the Bible? Do you no longer even believe in Jesus?"

This was precisely the kind of question I was not ready to answer, not to my mother especially. I adore my mom, and her opinion of me still matters as much as it did when I was a child. I told her – gently – that I wasn't "sure" if I still believed, hoping this half-lie would break the truth to her more gently.

Her response tore me up. It was exactly what I feared.

She was afraid for my soul. She was afraid for my kids' souls. She was unbearably aggrieved. She wondered where she had gone wrong raising me. I had just broken her heart.

I was heartbroken too. I never wanted to cause my mother that kind of pain. In the following weeks, I said nothing about religion to anyone. There was no way I could come out atheist now. If my mom had reacted that strongly, how strongly would everyone else react?

However, quickly another discussion broke out on Facebook, this time over marriage equality, or the bans on same-sex marriage. I made it clear that I was very much in favor of marriage equality, and this sparked much controversy. I received yet again more distressed texts from my mom. I had no choice but to speak to my mother about this. We finally had a face-to-face talk in which I assured her that my decision to leave Christianity had been made after years of careful consideration and that she had done nothing wrong to lead me to that decision. She assured me she'd never stop praying for me, and I told her I expected nothing less. We embraced. We are still extremely close, and I know she loves and accepts me just as I am no matter what.

I also received emails from my father-in-law in Scotland.

In some ways, his emails are even harder for me to respond to. We can't see each other in person and discuss things like normal. His first email was very difficult to read, for it was full of concern, not only for my soul and my family's souls, but also concern for how my viewpoints were causing pain to my family, my mom and dad in particular. He asked that I consider the damage I was doing, not only to those who loved me and feared for me, but the damage I was doing to my own soul. I've said before how much I respect and love my in-laws, and how much I love and respect my own parents. To be accused of not caring about or respecting them hurt. Since then, most of the emails have been similar to my dad's, trying to reason with me through apologetics. My mother-in-law is also aggrieved over our decision but keeps it to herself, offering us only gentle assurances of prayer. I truly hate causing so much pain and sadness. It's hard being too far away to talk about these things face-to-face.

One of the worst moments was with my grandpa at the nursing home.

For a while, on Wednesdays, before after-school commitments made it impossible, I would take the kids up to Papaw's nursing home to visit. I suspected my extended family knew by now that I was dangling over the pit of hell. My suspicions were confirmed one Wednesday afternoon when I arrived at the nursing home. I gave my Papaw a hug and started to sit down when he said, "I hear you've not been going to church!"

"No sir, I guess I haven't," I replied, feeling like a kid caught stealing a cookie.

"You need to be going to church! Them kids need to be going to church! You need to be taking them! Every week!"

"Yes sir, I know..."

"You know the Lord sees what's in your heart. You need to be getting right with the Lord!" He continued on for a little while about the state of my heart. I think I shrunk a couple of inches during his sermon. He does not know I am an atheist. I don't see why he ever needs to know.

The final step was to come out all the way. I debated whether this was necessary, but again, I needed to rip off that itchy tag once and for all. I published a portion of this book on my blog. I told the world that I was atheist.

The responses were overwhelmingly positive. I did get unfriended by a few people. I did get some messages from concerned family members and friends, some less gracious than others. Apart from these few exceptions though, I received almost universal encouragement from Christians and non-Christians alike. Many Christian friends contacted me with promises that they still loved and accepted me, atheist or not. Many more friends contacted me to say they too had experienced or were experiencing the same kind of things and thanked me for bravely sharing my story with the world, for showing them they were not alone. Their messages in return comforted me. I am not alone either.

That is what kept me writing this book, in spite of the painful memories it drudged up, the tears it produced, the emotional and tedious hours spent reading and rereading my own words, erasing them, questioning them, and walking away from them all together for weeks or months at a time, not wanting to walk through this dark forest again and again and again. I wrote this for my own healing, and in doing so, I have given myself so much closure, freedom, and peace. But I have also written this for everyone else out there who has suffered their own devastating loss of faith. It is my hand held out to yours, to assure you that you are not alone. And to offer you hope that the loss of faith is not just a death – it is a new beginning. When the flower withers and the last petal falls, we should remember that there is a seed buried deep inside that is now free to be released and to grow into something new and inconceivably beautiful.

Acknowledgements

THIS BOOK BEGAN ITS LIFE as a wee embryo of an article – only about a page and a half long. The title was "The Five Stages of Grief" but only included three stages, since I hadn't actually made it past the third yet. I wrote it for a blog that Jonathan Hays and I were planning on starting; an anonymous blog about religion and society which never came to fruition.

I sent the article to Jonathan for his opinion. He read it and said no. He said the story wasn't complete, that he suspected I had a lot more to say. I went back to the piece to flesh it out a little, expecting to maybe lengthen it to approximately five pages, but once I started writing, I just kept on and on… and a year and a half later this book happened. Turns out he was right.

So my first expression of enormous gratitude goes to Jonathan Hays, for if it hadn't been for your advice this book probably would never have been written, and thanks also for all the revisions, discussions, suggestions, and proofreading you provided along the way.

My other most sincere acknowledgment well-deservedly goes to my husband, Scott. Not only did he tell me repeatedly that I could and should keep writing this book, but he put up with all my moodiness while reliving old emotions, dealt with the kids' squabbles while my eyes and fingers were glued to my computer (oblivious to the goings-on around me), and all my late nights hidden away in my room, writing and ignoring the dishes piling up in the sink (which he ungrudgingly washed and put away). More importantly, I thank him for letting me share the intimate details of our shared life for the entire world to see, despite him being a very private person. Thank you for putting up with me all these years and sticking by me in our worst moments. I love you more than words can say. Husbands don't get better than you, Scott.

Further acknowledgements go to the various people who offered me so much help along the way. Thank you, Mhairu Hamilton, Karen Loethen, Tom Christian, Deena Riddle, Sarah Hays, Tim Schulte, Lynn Hazeslip (for introducing me to Tim Schulte), the MBB Facebook group, Katie Sonneman, Taylor Muse, Tommy Blank (and the rest of Quiet Company), and Hemant

Mehta for all the valuable and wonderful ways in which you helped me make this publication become a reality. And a massive thank you goes to my brother Daniel Arnold, for not only offering me vital feedback during the writing process and helping verify specific memories (since our own memories can sometimes tell tall tales) but also for adequately satisfying me that where name and place changes were necessary, I had obscured them well enough that even you did not know to whom or where they were referring. (Either that, or you have a poor memory.)

Finally, I would be remiss if I did not express my heartfelt gratitude to two more very deserving people: my mom and dad. Sadly, memoirs often contain stories that are painful or uncomfortable for parents to read, so I want to say from the bottom of my heart how much I love you both and how thankful I am that you raised me with so much integrity, love, and self-sacrifice. I only hope my children will grow up to say the same about me when they write their memoirs.

Appendix

All Scripture referenced throughout the book (with the exception of two) is from the Holy Bible, New International Version®, NIV® Copyright ©1973, 1978, 1984, 2011 by Biblica, Inc.® Used by permission. All rights reserved worldwide.

Other Scripture is quoted from the King James Version (KJV).

1 - James 2:17
    In the same way, faith by itself, if it is not accompanied by action, is dead.

2 - Matthew 6:24
    No one can serve two masters. Either you will hate the one and love the other, or you will be devoted to the one and despise the other. You cannot serve both God and money.

3 - Psalm 51:12 12
    Restore to me the joy of your salvation
    and grant me a willing spirit, to sustain me.

4 - 2 Corinthians 6:14
    Do not be yoked together with unbelievers. For what do righteousness and wickedness have in common? Or what fellowship can light have with darkness?

5 - Luke 22:19-20
    And he took bread, gave thanks and broke it, and gave it to them, saying, "This is my body given for you; do this in remembrance of me." In the same way, after the supper he took the cup, saying, "This cup is the new covenant in my blood, which is poured out for you."

6 - Matthew 24:36
    "But about that day or hour no one knows, not even the angels in heaven, nor the Son, but only the Father."

7 - *Matthew 24:30-34*
"Then will appear the sign of the Son of Man in heaven. And then all the peoples of the earth will mourn when they see the Son of Man coming on the clouds of heaven, with power and great glory. And he will send his angels with a loud trumpet call, and they will gather his elect from the four winds, from one end of the heavens to the other.

"Now learn this lesson from the fig tree: As soon as its twigs get tender and its leaves come out, you know that summer is near. Even so, when you see all these things, you know that it is near, right at the door. Truly I tell you, this generation will certainly not pass away until all these things have happened."

8 - *Matthew 7:23 (KJV)*
And then will I profess unto them, I never knew you: depart from me, ye that work iniquity.

9 - *John 6:66-68*
From this time many of his disciples turned back and no longer followed him.

"You do not want to leave too, do you?" Jesus asked the Twelve.

Simon Peter answered him, "Lord, to whom shall we go? You have the words of eternal life. We have come to believe and to know that you are the Holy One of God."

10 - *1 John 2:19*
"They went out from us, but they did not really belong to us. For if they had belonged to us, they would have remained with us; but their going showed that none of them belonged to us."

11 - *Isaiah 62:11 (KJV)*
Behold, the Lord hath proclaimed unto the end of the world, Say ye to the daughter of Zion, Behold, thy salvation cometh; behold, his reward is with him, and his work before him.

12 - *James 5:16*
Therefore confess your sins to each other and pray for each other so that you may be healed. The prayer of a righteous person is powerful and effective.

13 - *Matthew 13:24-30*
Jesus told them another parable: "The kingdom of heaven is like a man who sowed good seed in his field. But while everyone was sleeping, his enemy came and sowed weeds among the wheat, and went away. When the wheat sprouted and formed heads, then the weeds also appeared.

"The owner's servants came to him and said, 'Sir, didn't you sow good seed in your field? Where then did the weeds come from?'

"'An enemy did this,' he replied.

"The servants asked him, 'Do you want us to go and pull them up?'

"'No,' he answered, 'because while you are pulling the weeds, you may uproot the wheat with them. Let both grow together until the harvest. At that time I will tell the harvesters: First collect the weeds and tie them in bundles to be burned; then gather the wheat and bring it into my barn.'"

14 - 1 Corinthians 3:2

I gave you milk, not solid food, for you were not yet ready for it. Indeed, you are still not ready.

15 - Romans 8:38-39

For I am convinced that neither death nor life, neither angels nor demons, neither the present nor the future, nor any powers, neither height nor depth, nor anything else in all creation, will be able to separate us from the love of God that is in Christ Jesus our Lord.

16 - Matthew 13:18-23

"Listen then to what the parable of the sower means: When anyone hears the message about the kingdom and does not understand it, the evil one comes and snatches away what was sown in their heart. This is the seed sown along the path. The seed falling on rocky ground refers to someone who hears the word and at once receives it with joy. But since they have no root, they last only a short time. When trouble or persecution comes because of the word, they quickly fall away. The seed falling among the thorns refers to someone who hears the word, but the worries of this life and the deceitfulness of wealth choke the word, making it unfruitful. But the seed falling on good soil refers to someone who hears the word and understands it. This is the one who produces a crop, yielding a hundred, sixty or thirty times what was sown."

17 - 1 Corinthians 1:27

But God chose the foolish things of the world to shame the wise; God chose the weak things of the world to shame the strong.

18 - Proverbs 22:6

Start children off on the way they should go,
    and even when they are old they will not turn from it.

19 - Romans 8:26

In the same way, the Spirit helps us in our weakness. We do not know what we ought to pray for, but the Spirit himself intercedes for us through wordless groans.

20 - Matthew 7:7-11

"Ask and it will be given to you; seek and you will find; knock and the door will be opened to you. For everyone who asks receives; the one who seeks finds; and to the one who knocks, the door will be opened.

"Which of you, if your son asks for bread, will give him a stone? Or if he asks for a fish, will give him a snake? If you, then, though you are evil, know how to give good gifts to your children, how much more will your Father in heaven give good gifts to those who ask him!

21 - Joshua 24:15

"But if serving the Lord seems undesirable to you, then choose for yourselves this day whom you will serve, whether the gods your ancestors served beyond the Euphrates, or the gods of the Amorites, in whose land you are living. But as for me and my household, we will serve the Lord."

22 - 1 John 4:18

There is no fear in love. But perfect love drives out fear, because fear has to do with punishment. The one who fears is not made perfect in love.

23 - Hebrews 11:6

And without faith it is impossible to please God, because anyone who comes to him must believe that he exists and that he rewards those who earnestly seek him.

24 - Ephesians 2:8

For it is by grace you have been saved, through faith—and this is not from yourselves, it is the gift of God - not by works, so that no one can boast.

25 - Hebrews 11:6

And without faith it is impossible to please God, because anyone who comes to him must believe that he exists and that he rewards those who earnestly seek him.

26 - Malachi 1:2-3

"I have loved you," says the Lord.

"But you ask, 'How have you loved us?'

"Was not Esau Jacob's brother?" declares the Lord. "Yet I have loved Jacob, but Esau I have hated, and I have turned his hill country into a wasteland and left his inheritance to the desert jackals."

27 - James 1:6-7

But when you ask, you must believe and not doubt, because the one who doubts is like a wave of the sea, blown and tossed by the wind. That person should not expect to receive anything from the Lord.

About the Author

Lori Arnold McFarlane has a degree in English with a Creative Writing Emphasis from the University of Arkansas at Fayetteville, AR. She currently lives in Arkansas with her husband, three children, and two cats.

She blogs at www.scottandlori.com.

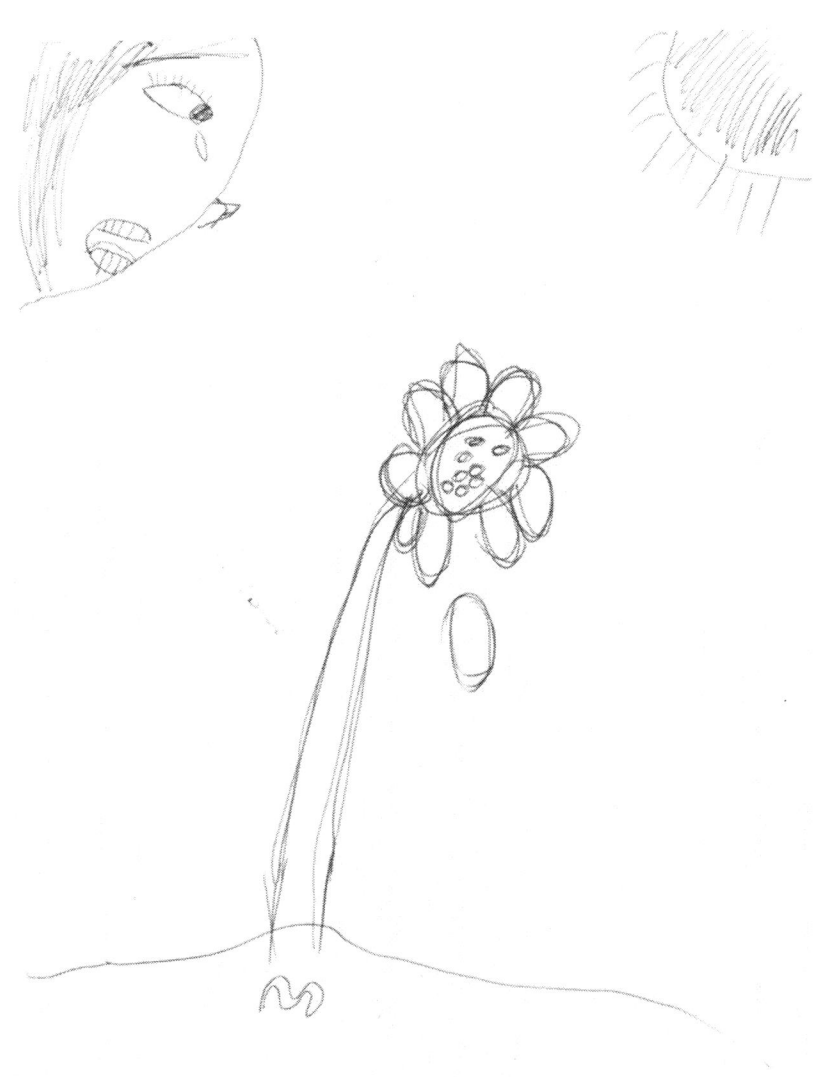

*Proposed cover design
by my daughter, Fi.*

Made in the USA
Lexington, KY
10 April 2016